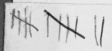

The Art of Magic

The automation of Maskelyne

The Art of
MAGIC

DOUGLAS AND KARI HUNT

ATHENEUM *1967* NEW YORK

To Melvin, Ruth, Herbert, and Nell

Contents

List of Illustrations

All Photographs Courtesy Koolkin

Magic and Conjuring

HUMAN BEINGS learn in two different ways. One is to observe nature directly and the other is to receive knowledge from others, usually in the form of symbols like words or pictures. In either case the information must be received through the senses of sight, hearing, taste, touch, and smell and then stored and interpreted by the mind.

Life would be simple, although unbearably dull, if all these processes operated perfectly. We all know that they do not. And for many reasons. The information we receive may be false. Or others may try to deceive us. And, of course, our imagination is generally less limited than our understanding. We may confuse symbols with real things. But most of all, our minds operate in a way determined by our evolutionary history as well as by our personal experiences. We learn to expect things to happen in a certain pattern and are surprised when they do not. We deceive ourselves because we see what we want to see or think we should see.

Throughout history there runs a thin thread of eccentrics who have studied the art of deception not to defraud but to put it in what they consider to be its proper place. Deception, they believe, does not belong in any of the serious and solemn areas of human thought and action. It should be used for entertainment, thereby reminding people, without harming them, that they can be deceived.

These students and practitioners of honest deception are known by many names, but most commonly they are known as magicians. This name is somewhat unfortunate because it is also used to refer to an ancient semi-religion whose followers purported to work miracles in order to exercise power over others. To clarify this confusion of symbols the English often refer to the entertainer magicians as conjurers. In ancient times they were often referred to as jugglers, but that word has now taken on a different meaning.

In this book, we will use the English terminology, and the word magician will refer to one who claims to do real miracles, and the word conjurer to one who practices deception openly to entertain and instruct.

Ancient magic was based on the theory that real things could be controlled by manipulating the symbols for them. This was such an attractive theory that it was invented by practically every primitive tribe that ever existed. If they could cause rain to fall by reciting a magic formula or by doing a symbolic rain dance then there would be no need to spend their time laboriously digging irrigation ditches. And if one could kill an enemy by sticking pins in a doll representing him, it would be foolish to challenge him to battle.

Different names were given to various branches of this theory of magic, depending upon whether the symbols manipulated were words, objects, or processes.

The magic of words was called incantation. It was thought that by uttering certain words and phrases it was possible to ward off danger, cure the sick, make people fall in love, and accomplish all manner of other things. Words can accomplish many of these things, but only if they communicate information from one person to another. Ancient magic held that the words could accomplish the things by themselves, which is quite another matter.

Both spoken and written words were thought to have magical power, although the spoken words had a special value because they could be sung or chanted. Some names were so powerful that it was forbidden to speak them. And it was thought to be possible to get rid of demons by repeating their names, omitting one sound in the name with each repetition until the demon shriveled away just like his name. Some ancient words of power, like abracadabra, derived from ancient Hebrew sources, have survived to the present day.

It was an easy step from belief in the magic powers of words to a belief in the magic powers of objects. Sometimes the object was given magical properties by simply writing magic words on it. Such a magical object is called a talisman, although not all talismans derived their alleged magic value from words. There were also talismans that were thought to have magic properties because they were made in the shape of deities or demons. The ancient Greeks also believed that precious and semiprecious stones had magic properties.

Sympathetic magic was the belief that a series of actions properly performed with available objects would induce somewhat similar actions to take place elsewhere. Thus, if the proper person took a mouthful of water under the right conditions and spit it on the ground, it would cause rain to fall. In ancient India it was thought possible to cure a fever by washing the victim and then pouring the wash water on a toad. The coolness of the toad would transfer itself to the fever victim.

There were many other varieties of ancient magic: necromancy, the communication with the dead; divination, or the predicting of future events; the summoning up of assorted demons and spirits; and alchemy, the search for magic methods to convert one substance into another.

Though, demonstrably, none of these assorted varieties of magic really worked, they became so powerful and widespread that their practitioners controlled the lives of millions of people over thousands of years of human history.

This happened because they sometimes seem to work. If you sit alongside a sick person beating on a tom-tom and chanting gibberish long enough, he may recover, just as he probably would if you had stayed away. Having succeeded in saving a patient, you may think that his cure was caused by your actions. If he believed wholeheartedly in your powers as a magician, your tom-tom solo may have actually had a positive effect on his recovery.

Sometimes the magical procedures worked simply because they were in accord with natural phenomena. The ancient Egyptian magicians went through a ceremony intended to cause the sun to rise in the morning. The sun never failed to rise, and the incantations used seemed to be eminently well suited to the job.

Sometimes the magicians discovered a scientific principle without realizing it. Digitalis, now used for some heart ailments, is a chemical produced by certain plants used by some witch doctors in making magic potions to treat heart patients.

Not all the unconscious discoveries made by the magicians were beneficial, however. Witches, or female magicians, used to meet in out of the way places for a ceremony called the sabbat. It is said that on these occasions they would dance, anoint themselves with magic ointments, summon up demons and even the devil, and then fly about the countryside. In understanding these reports it is helpful to know that the magic ointments included such ingredients as opium, hashish, and hemp. Some of the witches undoubtedly thought they had been flying.

But even if ancient magicians had never had any successes, they would have had some followers because most people confronted by a problem they don't know how to solve would rather do something than nothing. Magic at least had the virtue of promising some sort of results.

Later, when magicians learned to pay more attention to real things and relegated symbols to their proper place as a means of conveying information, the art of magic developed into science. Alchemy became chemistry, and astrology became astronomy. Even divination is being studied as extra-sensory perception.

But the individual magicians of long ago did not know that their art would eventually develop into something reliable. No matter how hard they worked to perfect their skills, their successes were largely accidental and therefore limited. Having promised to do the impossible, they were faced with the difficult problem of living up to their promise.

Their problem was especially acute because many of them had worked their way into positions of power as advisors to kings and pharaohs and other very important persons. Faced with a situation like this, it is not surprising that many of them became experts in deception.

Deception and Magic

SOME OF THE ancient magicians honestly believed in magic and devoted a tremendous amount of time and mental energy to the task of finding workable magic formulae.

There were other ancient magicians who were less honest, but more practical. They realized that their prestige and power depended not on miracles, which they found difficult to bring about, but on their ability to convince the general public that they could perform miracles.

These practical magicians built statues that were supposed to have the magical ability to speak. And speak they did, for the magicians built speaking tubes into the statues so someone could provide the voice from a concealed location.

Some people have deluded themselves into thinking that they have seen ghosts. And perhaps they do exist. But if they do, they are certainly shy and unreliable. So magicians found ways to make them appear reliably and on schedule. By concealing a concave mirror in a

9

position where it could project an image above a cere-
monial fire, they were able to produce ghostly figures
by throwing incense into the fire. The smoke rising
from the incense served as a screen on which the image
of a concealed "ghost" reflected by the mirror could be
seen.

Other magicians awed their followers by putting
wood on their altars and causing the wood to burst into
fire spontaneously as they recited magic words. This
was accomplished either by the use of chemicals or by
a sort of Molotov cocktail contained in the ashes already on the altar. A firebrand or a bit of glowing char-
coal was placed in a container with some highly in-
flammable material in such a way that when it was dis-
turbed it would soon burst into flame. When the wood
was thrown on the altar it jarred this incendiary container enough to start the fire.

Many pneumatic devices were constructed to produce effects that seemed miraculous. An air chamber
was constructed under the altar of one ancient temple
so that the doors would open magically when a fire was
built on the altar. The air in the chamber expanded
when heated and forced water through a pipe and into
a bucket that served as a counterweight for the door.
The water made the bucket heavier, the bucket de-
scended, and the door opened automatically.

At another temple an air chamber, open at the bottom, was suspended over water on a chain connected
to the temple doors. When the doors were opened, the
chain lengthened, the air chamber was lowered into the
water, air pressure was built up in the chamber until
it was strong enough to blow an attached trumpet.

More than one ancient temple had a miraculous

fountain that stayed full of water no matter how much was taken from it. In order to accomplish this apparent miracle the ancient magicians constructed a concealed pipeline from the fountain to a reservoir in another room. The unseen reservoir was kept filled to the desired level by the equivalent of the modern float valve. Since both the fountain seen by visitors to the temple and the concealed reservoir would maintain the same level of water the visible fountain did indeed hold the same amount of water no matter how much was taken from it. The float valve invented for this trick fountain has survived to the present day; it is now used in the flush tank of the household water closet.

While theoretical alchemists were explaining away their failure to make real gold from cheaper metals, practical alchemists discovered how to make gold alloys, which apparently increased the amount of gold, and invented gold plating, which enabled them to make other metals look like gold.

When it came to magic talismans, there were some that would bring good fortune to the bearer and others that would bring ill fortune. Sometimes these talismans worked because of their psychological effects on the bearer, but the magicians did not always rely on psychology. In one recently investigated case, some ancient magic statuettes were discovered to be made of arsenic sulphide, a deadly poison. They were thought to bring bad luck to anyone who handled them; and if the handler did not wash his hands before eating, they would have.

An Arab magician, Hassan Sabbah, the leader of the sect sometimes called the Assassins, secured the fanatical devotion of his followers by giving them a glimpse of Paradise. He accomplished this by drugging them and having them carried while unconscious to a garden of great beauty, well stocked with delicious fruits and other foods as well as many beautiful maidens. When they ate any of the fruit, which was drugged, they would fall back to sleep and he would have them carried back to the place where he had originally drugged them. When they awoke, he told them he had permitted them a short stay in the paradise that awaited them if they died in his service. His followers were famous for their complete lack of fear.

Thus in the East, the Near East, in Egypt, Greece, Rome, and Medieval Europe, magicians discovered the uses of deception. They made many technical discoveries without creating a science. Instead of using their knowledge to promote the general welfare, they kept most of their real knowledge secret and used it to create synthetic miracles and promote their own power.

Deception was not, of course, invented entirely by the magicians nor did it disappear from the earth when the ancient magicians lost their power over the minds of men.

There are advertising men today who, perhaps unwittingly, believe in the principles of ancient magic. They confuse symbols with things and show a picture of a beautiful girl to sell an automobile. Somewhat like Hassan Sabbah, they use television to drug their followers with entertainment and then show them a vision of the paradise they may inhabit if they will only use the right hair creme or mouthwash or soap.

The temple doors no longer swing open by magic. We know all about electric eyes and automatic door openers.

Yet deception to produce miracles is not unknown in our modern world. Not many years ago a company was prosecuted for selling a reducing drug that on analysis turned out to contain tapeworm eggs.

Some deception is done on a large scale, for deception is used in war. During the First World War the British Navy disguised warships as old tramp steamers in order to lure German submarines within striking distance. During the Second World War the invasion of France through Normandy by the Allies was covered by an elaborate campaign of deception to convince the Germans that the real attack was coming in another location.

Some criminals, particularly confidence men, are masters of deception. Two men dressed in work clothes once shoplifted a canoe from a New York department store. Although everyone in the store saw them take it, they naturally assumed the men were working for the store.

Entertainment is largely a matter of illusion and deception. When we see a play or a motion picture or a television show, we want to be deceived and transported into another world for the duration of the performance. The conjurer is of course a specialist within this world of entertainment. He tries to transport audiences into a special world where miracles happen.

The conjurer's purpose is to entertain, not to deceive. If he really meant to deceive his audience, he would not openly announce that he intended to deceive them. But the only way to create apparent miracles is to deceive, and the good conjurer is always on the watch for ingenious new developments in the field of deception. Over the centuries this has made the conjurer one of the most effective enemies of magic, dishonest gambling, spirit mediums, and all other forms of charlatanism.

The Methods of Deception

ALL DECEPTION, whether practiced by magician, crook, charlatan, or conjurer follows the same fundamental principles because its objective is the same: to mislead the mind of another human.

The most obvious way to fool another person is to lie to him. This is not only reprehensible, but it does not work very well. For it to be effective the listener must have confidence in the liar, and liars do not usually achieve the prestige one needs to inspire confidence. The conjurer of course cannot lie because he has told the audience in advance that he intends to fool them, and they therefore disbelieve anything he says anyway.

Suggestion is far more effective than direct misstatement. If a crook wants to sell a fake diamond ring, he must not dump it out of a box with fifty other similar rings, he must handle it as if it were valuable. If a conjurer wants to convince his audience that his hands are empty when in fact they are not, he cannot tell the audience he has nothing in his hands. This only

15

attracts attention to a place where he does not want attention. Instead he must handle his hands as if they are empty.

Sometimes suggestion can be built into the apparatus used by a conjurer. A famous trick of the vaudeville era was the vanish of a duck performed by a conjurer named Nixon. The duck was placed in a box on a table and then the box was dismantled piece by piece. This left no apparent hiding place but the table, so the conjurer next dismantled the table showing that the duck was not there either. Actually the duck was concealed in one section of the box. The table was provided with a projecting duck feather, which came into view when the duck was first placed in the box. This suggested to the audience that the duck was actually hidden in the table. Because the audience's attention was on the table and not on the box, they were not watching closely when the duck was taken away with one section of the box. Instead, they were surprised when the conjurer tipped the table over and showed that it was only an empty frame.

More frequently, however, the suggestions that mislead the spectator must be provided by the acting skill of the conjurer. This is the skill that the average conjurer lacks most. To be a good conjurer one must not only possess the actor's ability to sell what one is playing, but one must be able to sense what the audience is thinking and offset it by action and words.

To understand anything, an individual must observe all the relevant facts and then devote his full attention to understanding the relationship between the facts. To deceive someone it is necessary to prevent this process from being carried out. One way to do this is to provide a distraction, something else for the person to think about. The confidence man does this by getting his victim to think about the profit he, the victim, is going to make out of the con man's scheme. This prevents the victim from thinking rationally about the scheme.

The magicians evolved such elaborate systems of signs and symbols and incantations and talismans that their followers never really investigated their basic assumptions nor their synthetic miracles.

Conjurers use the same basic technique of distraction. If the conjuring trick is made sufficiently interesting, the spectator does not think about how it is accomplished until it is too late for him to observe carefully. Sometimes the distractions used by conjurers are remarkably direct. In vanishing a girl from an oversize cannon on stage, one conjurer loaded the cannon with a large rubber ball as well as the girl. After the cannon was fired, the ball flew out into the audience. It was difficult for the audience not to follow the flight of the apparent cannon ball, and this distraction gave the girl time to make her getaway from her hiding place in the cannon.

Anything significantly different from the normal attracts attention. Anything apparently normal tends to be invisible. Several years ago a restaurant proprietor in New York had a wooden fire plug made, which he used to save himself a parking space near his restaurant. He left the false fire hydrant at the curb when he was using his car, and when he returned, he parked and put the hydrant inside. Neither the police nor the fire department noticed this, nor did the motorists who carefully avoided parking within ten feet of the hydrant. Not until one motorist did park in front of the fake hydrant and was given a parking ticket was attention drawn to the hydrant and the trick discovered.

Disguise is also essential to the conjurer. Some of the best conjuring is done with normal everyday articles like coins and cards and rope. When any article to be used must be faked in some way, it is desirable that it look like an everyday article in order not to cause suspicion although sometimes this rule is hard to follow. A box to hold a woman who is to be sawed in half is not an everyday article no matter how it's decorated.

Sometimes conjuring apparatus is designed to look like an everyday article in the time and place of its origin, but the design tends to become immortal and is used long after its prototypes have become antiques. You may still see performers doing tricks with nineteenth century English household items like tea caddies and egg cups, now frequently decorated with Chinese lettering.

Still another way to deceive is to withhold information. This was the chief method used by the ancient magicians. Many new technical discoveries can look like magic if they are presented without explanation, or with a false explanation and are surrounded with an air of mystery. By keeping their scientific discoveries secret, the ancient magicians held back the progress of science but were able to create apparent miracles.

Conjurers too have withheld information in order to deceive people, but only in fun. Possibly because, unlike the magicians, conjurers have never had any power, the secrets of conjuring have never been as well concealed as those of the magicians. It has always been possible for anyone with a genuine interest in conjuring to learn the art.

Conjurers have always taken advantage of the latest scientific discoveries, discoveries their audiences would not know about or would not understand, whenever it has been possible to present them in an entertaining manner. In the early days of the scientific revolution conjurers frequently presented elaborate mechanical devices to their audiences. Conjuring tricks with a scientific basis became very popular and undoubtedly helped create interest in science before science had become powerful enough to revolutionize the world.

Confusion can also be used to deceive. This is probably of more use to a criminal than it is to a conjurer, for generally to entertain an audience a conjurer must do apparently impossible things without confusing them. The best deception occurs when apparently pains have been taken to prevent deception. Nevertheless some kinds of confusion can cover some kinds of action.

The conjurer's miracles must seem to really be miracles accomplished naturally and as a part of life. If all the means of deception are well used, the conjurer can easily create puzzles for his audience, but this is not enough. The conjurer must, like all performers, convey thoughts and emotions to his audience. The playlets he presents must be more than puzzles. They must have a dramatic climax in which the audience is swept up into what is happening. The conjurer must create illusion.

Illusion

CONJURING illusion is created by using methods of deception to create in the mind of a spectator a false understanding of what is happening before him and then, in an entertaining way, showing him that he has been mistaken in his analysis of the situation.

There are many natural illusions that do the same thing. Although they are not often of direct use to a conjurer, a knowledge of them is a great aid in understanding conjuring.

One of the earliest illusions to be recognized as such is the one shown on page 23. If you cross two fingers, as shown in the illustration, and bring both of them in contact with a marble, then roll the marble about under the fingers, keeping both fingers in contact with the marble, you will apparently feel two marbles rather than one. The illusion fools only the unconscious part of your mind, for you know quite well with the thinking part of your mind that there is only one marble there. You can even look at the marble as you roll it, and although your eyes tell you there is only one, your

20

mind will keep on telling you, misinformed by its sense of touch, that there are two.

The marble creates an illusion of touch. But the most interesting illusions are those that reach the mind through the eye. There are illusionists who appeal first to the ear, but they are called ventriloquists rather than conjurers. And even in this highly specialized field a great deal depends on the visual illusion of a dummy talking. The conjurer's strongest appeal is to the eye, and he must concentrate on making his performance entertaining to the eye.

What the mind sees is not the same thing as what the eye sees. If you hold one hand eight or ten inches from your eyes and hold the other hand at arm's length you will find that they look the same size. Naturally? No, not at all. The near one should look much larger than the far one because the image in your eye of the near one is much larger than that of the far one. In a photograph the near one would look much larger. But your mind knows that both hands are the same size, and it insists on seeing them that way even if your thinking mind knows that they should look different.

This non-thinking part of your mind that interprets visual images is a very remarkable instrument. Some of the things it does can only be explained by saying that it has learned, during millions of years of evolution, to use the information it receives in ways that help the individual survive in a hostile world. For this reason its attention is directed to moving objects in preference to stationary ones. Moving objects are more likely to be dangerous. If the information given it is incomplete, it tries to fill in the missing parts. For example, when you see a shadow of something you tend to see the object itself. When the information your eye receives can be interpreted in two ways, your mind automatically chooses what it has learned to be the most likely interpretation. For example, if you are sitting in a train and the train on the next track begins to move in a direction opposite to that in which you expect to go, it is almost impossible to overcome the feeling that you are moving forward, even though your train is stationary. All you can see of the outside world is the other train and your mind knows it is more likely that you are moving than that the outside world should be moving by; therefore it assumes that you must be moving, and insists on telling you so even though you know better.

The non-thinking part of your mind can become confused by being given more information than it needs, more information than it can handle or the same information for too long a time. If you look at a very repetitive drawing, as on page 23, you will feel a certain confusion because the drawing gives you the same information more times than you need, to know what kind of pattern it is.

Some illusions can be dangerous. When one is driving a car at night on a modern highway, one's mind can become tired and begin to consider the car as the stationary object and the small white line that divides the highway lanes as the moving object. An airplane pilot landing his plane can be misled if the lights at the far end of the runway are brighter than those at the near end. He then sees the runway in reverse and is likely to make a fatal error. People who have lived in forests have trouble adjusting their perceptions when they move to an area where distant vision is possible.

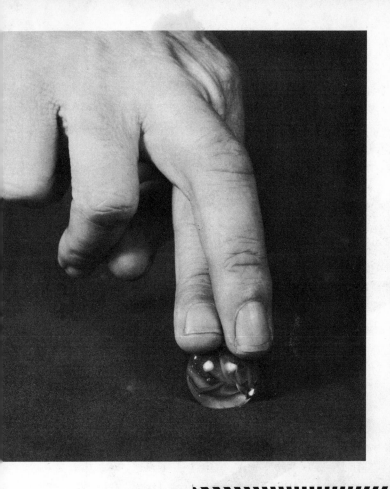

From *Eye and Brain* by R. L.
Gregory. Copyright © 1966 by
R. L. Gregory. Used by permission
of McGraw-Hill Book Company.

Pictures courtesy L. S. and R. Penrose
and *British Journal of Psychology*.

Space will have more than its share of optical illusions because the seeing part of the mind, which is so stubborn about telling the thinking part of the mind what it has learned over millions of years, will have had no time to learn how things should look in a totally new environment.

This suggests one reason why man is so interested in illusion. Unlike lower species, man is continually creating new situations for himself and he must continually fight against seeing these new situations with perceptions developed a million years ago. Sometimes he invents scientific ways to improve his perceptions. Sometimes he takes advantage of their defects, as in the illusion of motion pictures. A series of pictures projected in sequence with the right timing will give an illusion of continuous movement. The mind fills in the movement that is not there in the actual pictures. Timing in this illusion is very important. At thirty frames per second the illusion of motion exists, but it flickers preceptibly. At fifty frames per second it seems to be smooth. Often in conjuring this same matter of timing is important in creating illusion. When a trick consists of the magical transport of an article from one place to another, one particular distance between the place the item vanishes from and the place it reappears at, and one length of time between the vanishing and the reappearance will produce the maximum effect. If the timing or spacing is poor, the trick will look like the vanishing of one article and the production of another.

Some illusions cannot be avoided, others must be learned. The ability to see depth in a flat picture or drawing is something that every civilized person learns.

But it is an illusion and was invented rather late in human history. Even people as clever as the ancient Egyptians never thought of trying to give an illusion of depth to their paintings. Most people do not realize how much of an illusion pictures are because they learned to see them in the accepted manner at a very early age. If you do not believe that the representation of three dimensional things on flat paper is artificial and an illusion, look at page 24 and try to imagine yourself walking down the flight of stairs in the drawing. You will find that you walk down the steps endlessly but end up at the same point all the time, which you know is impossible.

In bullfighting there is a "moment of truth." In photography there is, according to famous photographer Henri Cartier-Bresson, a "decisive moment" when the picture must be taken. In the best conjuring tricks there is a critical moment when the seeing part of the mind of the spectator realizes that it is seeing something that cannot be. These tricks survive as classics of conjuring even when most of the audience knows how they are done. The Chinese Linking Ring trick, which is familiar to almost everyone, has two such moments. One is when the rings are struck together and joined, and the other is when two of the rings are separated by pulling one slowly through the other. The actual manipulation is done before the illusionary moment. The rings are separated before they are drawn slowly past each other to simulate the passage of one through the other. But even although the thinking mind knows that one ring has an opening in it, and may even know exactly how it is all done, the illusion of passing solid steel through solid steel is powerful enough to make the trick effective.

Most natural illusions and some classics of conjuring retain their illusionary quality even when the viewer knows how they are accomplished, but most conjuring feats need the element of surprise to create an illusion. An old conjuring rule says that a trick should never be repeated for the same audience, particularly on the same occasion. The second time around the element of surprise is completely lacking.

Egypt and Magic

THERE ARE those who think that illusion was first discovered by man when he noticed that the moon looks larger near the horizon than it does overhead. There are those who think that conjuring, in the sense of illusion created by deception, was invented by some unknown primitive man who discovered that he could pretend to put a pebble in his hand and then make it apparently vanish by simply opening his hand. And then there are those who believe that everything was invented in ancient Egypt.

Magic, to the ancient Egyptians, was more important than life itself. Magical symbols in the form of words and objects were placed in tombs to serve the dead. They believed so firmly that symbols had a life of their own that when they wrote the symbols for dangerous animals they often wrote them in mutilated form so the animals they symbolized could not harm anyone.

They built great temples in which priests and magicians could carry on their mysteries. Some of these temples were so large that some of our most famous modern buildings could be placed inside them. Their temples were not like our churches, and their priest-magicians were not like our clergy. The Egyptian temples and attendants were there to care for the magical symbols of the gods; this had to be done well to insure that the universe ran properly.

Egyptian magic controlled the lives of the people of Egypt for thousands of years; and after Egyptian civilization withered away, their magic lived on in customs and superstitions. Even today traces of it may be found in unexpected places. Have you ever noticed that there is an Egyptian magic symbol on our one dollar bill?

Because of the use of magic in Egypt it is often claimed that conjuring began in Egypt. But a conjurer is not a magician. To show that conjuring began in Egypt, we would have to show that there were performers in ancient Egypt who performed their miracles for entertainment. We know that ancient Egypt had singers, harp players, lute players, lyre players, trumpeters, flute players, drummers, acrobatic dancers, mimes, exotic dancers, animal trainers, wrestlers, boomerang throwers, bull fighters, gymnasts, prize fighters, jugglers, and poets.

But no conjurers. At least the evidence for them is very slim. There is a drawing in a tomb at Beni Hassan, halfway between Cairo and Luxor, that is thought by some to be a representation of two conjurers performing the cups and balls trick, but there are other authorities who say it is a drawing of two men playing some sort of now forgotten game.

Probably the ancient Egyptians believed too sincerely in magic to tolerate very much conjuring. Performing admittedly fake miracles in Egypt would have been about as popular as a joke book about the Einstein theory would be now.

The only real evidence that conjuring may have been known in ancient Egypt is in fiction. There is an Egyptian story written almost 3000 years ago that may have been based on a conjuring performance, may have been based on things done by the magicians, or may have been purely imaginative.

The story is contained in a document known as the Westcar Papyrus written around 1700 B.C. in Egypt, discovered about 150 years ago, and last heard of in Berlin just before the Second World War. The papyrus tells the story of a magician, Dedi, who lived during the time of the Pharaoh Kheops (about 2900 B.C.) and about two other magicians of still earlier date.

In the tale related by the papyrus, Kheops is being entertained by some of the princes of the realm. Prince Khephren tells about a magician, Ubaoner, who lived in the time of King Nebka. Ubaoner disposed of an unfaithful servant by making a wax crocodile and then by magic changing the wax beast into a real live crocodile twelve feet long, which dragged the servant to the bottom of a pond.

Next Prince Baufre tells the Pharaoh a story of the magician Zazamonkh, who lived in the time of King Snefru. Snefru was watching some of his most beautiful female attendants rowing boats about the palace lake when one of them lost a malachite pendant. The King offered to replace it, but the girl wanted her original pendant; so Zazamonkh folded the water of the lake over, as one would close an open book, and found the pendant on the bottom of the lake.

After this, Prince Hardahaf tells the Pharaoh of a living magician, Dedi, who, although his age was a hundred and ten, ate five hundred loaves of bread, a haunch of beef, and one hundred jugs of beer a day. Dedi, the princes said, knew how to make a lion follow him without a leash, and how to restore to its rightful place a head that had been cut off. The Pharaoh was very much interested in this account of the magician and ordered Dedi to be brought to the court to demonstrate his skill. Immediately a mission headed by Prince Hardahaf was sent to bring the magician from Ded-Snefru.

When Dedi was brought into the hall of the palace, the Pharaoh asked him, "Why is it that I have never seen you before?"

Dedi replied, "Because you did not send for me before."

The king chose to ignore this remark and said, "I understand you can restore a head that has been cut off."

"Yes, that is true, your majesty."

"Bring in one of the prisoners," commanded the Pharaoh.

"That will not be necessary, your majesty, let me demonstrate with one of the lower, but still excellent animals."

So saying, Dedi cut the head off a goose and then replaced it on the body of the goose, said some magic words, and the goose cackled and was whole again. The Pharaoh was so impressed that he requested it be done again. Dedi complied by cutting off the head of a duck and restoring it, just as he had done the goose. Again the Pharaoh requested a repeat performance. This time Dedi cut off the head of a bull and restored it.

The Pharaoh was by this time so impressed with Dedi's power that he requested him to make a prophecy. Dedi, possibly still annoyed that the Pharaoh had not sent for him until he was a hundred and ten years old, prophesied the end of the Pharaoh's reign and the founding of a new dynasty.

Some authorities have said that this story shows that ancient Egypt had conjurers who knew how to perform decapitation tricks. Many magicians during the middle ages and later performed the trick of apparently decapitating a bird and restoring the head. It was usually done by holding the real head of the bird back under its wing and tearing off a false head. The false head could then be vanished and the bird restored to its normal state.

The decapitation of a human being has also been performed for many hundreds of years. In medieval times it was done by placing the victim on a table with a secret opening. The real head was bent back through the opening, and a false head was cut off with a knife.

Whether the ancient Egyptians knew tricks of this sort or whether the decapitations in the story were as imaginary as the folding over of the lake will probably never be known.

Greece and Rome

CONJURING, as we know it today, probably began in ancient Greece. This is not too surprising since the theater as we know it was also invented in ancient Greece.

The Greek temperament and the Greek mind were suited to conjuring. The Greeks believed in reason, not magic. They did not think of truth as something handed down by those in authority but as something to be sought for by the individual. They looked for order in the universe, and were always interested when they saw an apparent paradox.

The Greeks also admired skill, both of the body and of the mind. They found joy in both physical and mental activity.

It was only natural then that the Greeks should be interested in skillfully performed miracles, done just for the fun of it. Many ancient Greek writers mention conjurers, and it is quite clear that the people referred to were entertainers and not magicians pretending real miracles.

A learned man, Athenaeus, edited a monumental work called *The Banquet of the Sages* in 228 A.D. This book contains excerpts from about fifteen hundred earlier books, and some of the excerpts mention conjurers. Curiously enough, although the *Banquet of the Sages* mentions many conjurers by name, it fails to tell anything about them or their performances. But then it gives us the first detailed and undeniably accurate description of a conjuring performance without telling us the name of the man who performed.

The account is taken from the works of a Greek author of the second century, Alciphron. It describes the classic sleight of hand trick known as the cups and balls and tells us that the performer was even more dexterous than Eurybates of Oechalia, "of whom we have heard so much."

The cups and balls trick is thought by most authorities to be the most fundamental of all conjuring tricks. It is so basic that it has been invented independently by performers in many different lands, and has survived with very little change through thousands of years. It is still performed by street conjurers in Egypt and India as well as by the most sophisticated American and European conjurers.

The effect of the trick is still the same as it was when Alciphron described it. Small balls, placed under inverted cups or dishes defy the laws of nature. They seem to travel mysteriously from one cup to another. When placed under separate cups one at a time, they cluster together under one of the cups. When they are all placed under one of the cups, they disperse and are found under separate cups. They pass mysteriously through the solid bottoms of the cups, they multiply, they even change into entirely different objects. Sometimes for a climax they change into potatoes or other vegetables, sometimes into large rubber balls, sometimes into live, baby chickens, sometimes even into wine glasses filled with liquid.

The very word used to designate a conjurer in many languages is derived from the cups and balls trick. The old French word for a conjurer was *escamoteur,* derived from the word *escamote,* the French version of the Arab word for a small cork ball, often used in the trick. The Greeks themselves called a conjurer *psephopaiktes,* from the Greek word for pebble; for the Greek sleight of hand performers used small pebbles instead of balls to perform the trick.

Having invented, or possibly having learned from some still older civilization, the cups and balls, it is probable that the Greeks developed other sleight of hand tricks. The cups and balls trick includes vanishings, appearances, transpositions, transformations, multiplication, and penetration. It is probable that intelligent people would have adapted these fundamental magical effects to other objects, but we have very little information about other sleight of hand effects in ancient Greece.

We know that Greek conjurers had many ingenious mechanical effects. Heron of Alexandria, who wrote extensively on technical subjects like hydraulics and pneumatics in the second century B.C., described many ingenious devices for entertainment and also described some of the deceptions used by the temple priests of Greece and Egypt.

Heron described a method of suspending a ball in the air by means of air pressure. You may be familiar with the modern version of this, which is a sort of bubble pipe through which you blow and support a light plastic ball in the air. Another ingenious device was a mechanical horse that had a rotating cam connection between the head and the body, arranged so that a sword could be passed completely through the neck of the horse without severing the head.

Among other things described by Heron were a mysterious drinking horn that would pour either water or wine at the pleasure of the person exhibiting it, and a sphere that would spin rapidly when heated. This last operated on the same basic principle as the steam turbines that supply much of our electric power.

Perhaps the most spectacular contraption described by Heron was a miniature theater that rolled out on stage by itself, stopped at the proper spot on stage, exhibited three magical tableaux performed by automata, then rolled off stage by itself.

Through other writings we read of other mechanical devices that were used in the Greek theater to create magical effects. Not all were used just in conjuring performances. Some of the stage directions for Greek plays call for characters to vanish or to appear suddenly or to float through the air. Unfortunately there were few technical writers like Heron, so although we know that the illusions were created, we do not know how they were done.

Rome too had its conjurers, but they do not seem to have achieved any great fame, nor did they develop anything that was an improvement on Greek magic.

The chief trick of the sleight of hand performers in Rome continued to be the cups and balls. This is evident from the name by which they were known, *acetabularii*, from *acetabulum*, the Latin word for a small cup used to contain vinegar.

Although large and spectacular stage effects were one of the main components of Roman theater, illusions do not seem to have been a major factor. A society that could present real executions, real massacres, and even real naval battles in its theaters was not particularly interested in illusion. Sawing a woman in half might have been considered entertainment by the Romans, but they would have been disappointed to find that she was restored at the end of the trick.

The main contribution of Rome to the theater was in spreading Greek theater to Africa, the Near East, and the remainder of Europe. After the fall of Rome and the disappearance of spectacular entertainment, the Greek and Roman mimes, jugglers, dancers, singers, and conjurers wandered over the known world and kept alive the traditions of the theater.

Early Hocus Pocus

THROUGHOUT the Middle Ages three streams of deception continued to flow. Conjurers wandered from place to place performing sleight of hand and relatively simple mechanical tricks; magicians made a religion out of their seeming ability to summon up the devil and his subordinate demons; and charlatans used the methods of both to take money and power from the unwary.

Although we know that conjurers traveled about Europe in Mediaeval times performing with acrobats, singers, jugglers, and mimes in market places, we know very little about their performances or their methods before the sixteenth century. But then several books were published that explained conjuring tricks in order to combat the prevalent, superstitious belief in black magic and charlatanry. The most famous of these books, at least in the English speaking world, was *Discoverie of Witchcraft* by Reginald Scot. In this book Scot proposed to reveal the "vertue and power of naturall magike," and explained a number

38

of conjuring feats of his day. For hundreds of years other authors borrowed Scot's material for books on conjuring, and Scot's book itself is still in print, almost four hundred years after it was written.

Although only a small part of Scot's book was devoted to conjuring, he explained such tricks as: burning a card and reproducing it from the pocket of a spectator; passing a coin from one pocket to another; making a coin pass through the table; making a coin vanish from a handkerchief; removing beads from a string while the ends of the string are held by a spectator; burning a thread and making it whole again; the cups and balls; the cut and restored cord; and cutting off a person's head and restoring it to its former position.

Scot, however, made no real attempt to teach anyone how to do conjuring; that was not his purpose in writing the book. The first important book in English to attempt to teach conjuring was *Hocus Pocus Jr., the Anatomy of Legerdemain,* published in 1634. No author's name is given on the title page of the book, and there are some authorities who think that Hocus Pocus Jr. was the pen name of the author rather than part of the title. This would provide an explanation of the origin of the term Hocus Pocus, which is otherwise a rather mysterious group of nonsense syllables used to refer to conjuring.

The book leans heavily on Scot, but introduces many illustrations and much material that is not in Scot. The unknown author of the book was trying to write a how-to-do-it book, though probably few people, if any, could really learn to do conjuring from it. The book made two errors, errors that have plagued text-books on conjuring ever since. The first was to assume that the only important part of a trick is the technical method employed. This is equivalent to telling someone that to play the violin one simply holds it against the neck with the left hand and scrapes the bow over the strings with the right hand. The second error was to try to give confidence to the prospective student by telling him that little knowledge, intelligence, skill, or practice were required to fool an audience. This is an opinion often held by a person who has learned something about the methods of conjuring, but has not learned that acting skill is also required. One author of books on conjuring was completely astounded to see some of the material he had described in print performed by a truly expert magician. He refused to believe that the magic was done in the way he himself had described it, although it actually was. Nevertheless, *Hocus Pocus Jr.* was a remarkable achievement for its time. The tricks in the book are presumably those of the itinerant conjurers. They include the cut and restored cord, coins passed through a table, the feat of passing a beer glass through a table, the vanishing of a card and its reappearance in a nut, the vanishing of a doll, and of course the cups and balls. Any of these feats, when well done, will entertain and fool a modern audience even in the atomic age.

Technology changes rapidly, but people do not. The old conjuring feats well performed will still fool an audience that is not too familiar with them, and for the same reason: because the good conjurer has a practical, working knowledge of psychology. The old conjurers did not know how to explain their knowledge; they had no specialized terms to set it down

L'Escamoteur by Jerome Bosch.

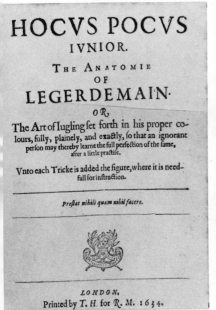

Title page and illustration from *The Anatomie of Legerdemain.*

with, but it is hard to surpass, for brevity at least, the following description of a magician given by *Hocus Pocus Jr.*

"First, he must be one of an impudent and audacious spirit, so that he may set a good face upon the matter.

Secondly, he must have a nimble and cleanly conveyance.

Thirdly, he must have strange terms, and emphatical words; to grace and adorn his actions, and the more, to astonish the beholders.

Fourthly, and lastly, such gestures of body as may lead away the spectators' eyes from a strict and diligent beholding his manner of conveyance."

Cagliostro and Pinetti

As the author of *Hocus Pocus Jr.* very wisely said, "The end of this Art is either good or bad, accordingly as it is used." Until the eighteenth century it was not realized that the principles of deception are the same whether they are used for charlatanry, conjuring, or purported black magic. Reginald Scot had attempted to point out the differences between conjuring and magic, but it remained for two very dramatic men to focus the attention of the dawning scientific age on the problems of trickery. These two men were Joseph Balsamo, the last of the great charlatans, and Joseph Pinetti de Willedal, the first of the great conjurers.

Joseph Balsamo, better known by his self-assumed title, Count de Cagliostro, was a man of such great energy, intelligence, and imagination that he could have become famous in a hundred different ways. Unfortunately he belonged to that small and incomprehensible group of humans who would rather win by cheating than by talent, and who would rather lie than breathe. He began his career by being driven from

43

a monastery for incorrigibility and ended it in a dungeon under a sentence of life imprisonment, after having been driven out of most of the capitals of Europe. But between these two events he blazed a trail of imaginative dishonesty through the most sophisticated peoples in the world.

Balsamo conjured up visions of the dead, made, or at least seemed to make, synthetic gold and synthetic diamonds, predicted the future, cured the sick, and invented the Egyptian rite of Masonry with himself, of course as the Grand Master. He dressed in the richest of robes and lived in a magnificent house furnished for him by the Cardinal de Rohan, whom he cheated out of a great deal of money. He claimed to possess the secret of eternal youth, and to prove it pointed to his beautiful wife, who he said was over sixty years of age. She was actually in her twenties. He was fawned upon by aristocrats and royalty as well as by screaming mobs of common people.

He accomplished all these things in a very dramatic way, using personality, bluff, the psychology of deception, sleight of hand, and a complete lack of a conscience. He was possibly the cleverest charlatan who ever lived. But he was always caught.

He was so flamboyantly clever and dishonest that he gave a bad reputation to charlatanry. In a way he accomplished what Reginald Scot had tried to do. He made it obvious that the summoning up of spirits, the prediction of the future, the magical conversion of base metals into gold, and many other things previously thought to be supernatural were actually clever frauds.

From Cagliostro's time on it became increasingly

necessary for charlatans and confidence men to give a pseudoscientific aura to their deceptions. The creation of miracles by the agency of magic words and stage-craft became purely a matter of entertainment.

Joseph Pinetti de Willedal was in many respects similar to Count de Cagliostro. He had the same sort of talent for fooling people that Cagliostro possessed, but he devoted himself to entertaining people, not to cheating them. Like Balsamo he gave himself a title, or rather he gave himself many titles. In one case he advertised himself as

"Chevalier M. Jean-Joseph Pinetti Willedale de Merci, Knight of the German Order of Merit of St. Philip, professor of mathematics and natural philosophy, pensioned by the Court of Prussia, patronized by all the Royal Family of France, aggregate of the Royal Academy of Sciences and Belles Lettres of Bordeaux, etc."

Although most of the Chevalier's titles were false, his talent for performing was real, and he was invited to perform before royalty on many occasions. He created a sensation at the court of Louis XVI of France by removing the shirt of a man in the audience without removing the gentleman's coat. To gain the approval of the most sophisticated audience in the world with such an inherently crude trick must have required a performing personality of the highest order.

Pinetti used an elaborate stage setting, very unlike the simple bag of tricks the wandering conjurers of the Middle Ages carried. The stage itself was covered with a beautiful rug. Downstage were two massive tables covered with scarlet cloths embroidered in gold and silver. To the rear of the stage was a very long table set with candelabra and the apparatus to be used in the performance. Above the stage hung an immense and elaborate chandelier with many candles.

Pinetti's repertoire of magic, which included many items of his own invention, was very wide. He would exhibit an empty box; this was placed closed in view of the audience, and then he would borrow a ring from a lady. The ring was placed in a pistol and fired at the box, which when opened was found to contain a dove with the ring in its beak. Pinetti would then walk into the audience with the dove and try to present the ring to a lady other than the owner; but the dove would shake its head and refuse to hand over the ring until it came to the real owner. At the real owner, the dove would voluntarily drop the ring. On one occasion when performing near the seashore, Pinetti substituted a fish for the dove, but there is no record of whether or not the fish exercised the same discretion as the dove in the return of the ring.

Pinetti did escape tricks over a hundred years before Harry Houdini made this type of magic the sensation of show business. Pinetti had his thumbs tied with cord and his hands covered with a hat; instantly he reached one hand out of concealment to drink a glass of wine, then throw the glass to the ceiling where it changed to confetti. When the audience looked back to his hands, they were already as securely tied as at the beginning. This same trick was later introduced as a Japanese mystery by a famous vaudeville performer named Ten-Ichi, although Ten-Ichi used Japanese paper rather than cord, and caught hoops on his arms while his thumbs were apparently securely tied.

Pinetti pins a card to a wall with a gun shot.

Fundamentally though the trick was the same, that is the instantaneous release of the bound thumbs. In many cases the dramatic presentation of a trick may be varied a great deal although the technical means of accomplishing it remains the same.

Automata, mechanical devices that imitate living things in some way, were constructed by the ancient Greeks and Egyptians and have fascinated mankind ever since. There are two types of automata. The first type is the real automaton, a clever mechanical device that does something it was programmed to do at the time of its assembly. An example of this type of automaton is the cuckoo clock. Pinetti was very clever with the other type of automaton, the so-called false automaton. He constructed a mechanical bird, which when placed on a flask on his table would not only flap its wings but would chirp out any tune the audience requested. The audience would have been less enchanted with this bird had it known that the sounds were produced by Pinetti's assistant warbling bird calls through a speaking trumpet to conceal their point of origin. Knowing this makes the trick seem absurdly simple, but it is not. It requires acting ability to convince an audience that a mechanical bird is obeying their spoken requests.

Pinetti was also the first to perform what is now known as the "second sight" act. The lady assistant sits on stage with a blindfold over her eyes and describes articles handed to the performer, who is walking around out in the auditorium. This type of performance has a certain similarity to some performances with false automata. The secret is in establishing some secret means of communication between the performer and the assistant. Sometimes the communication is concealed in the questions asked of the assistant by the performer. The performer, holding the article handed him by someone in the audience, chooses his words, sentence structure, and sometimes even the pauses and emphasis in his question according to a code known also to the assistant. After long and difficult practice it is possible to become so clever at this that it is hard to believe that what sounds like normal conversation is really a form of secret communication.

It is not known exactly what method Pinetti used, but he performed the trick so well that many people began to think that he and his wife did the second sight performance by some supernatural means.

In 1774 Pinetti wrote a book on his methods of conjuring. Unfortunately the book explained very little besides his method of doing the shirt removing trick. This sort of thing was characteristic of books on conjuring written by professional magicians until recently. Now there is a standard joke among magicians that the best way to hide a secret is to publish it in a highly technical book, and no one will pay any attention to it. Because Pinetti's book was so incomplete, an amateur magician, Henri Decremps of the Museum of Paris, wrote a book on conjuring in which he endeavored to explain many of Pinetti's methods.

This book, *La Magie Blanche Devoilée*, did not exactly cement friendly relations between Pinetti and Decremps. In revenge for the exposure of his material, Pinetti hired a seedy and disreputable looking man to sit in the audience at each of his performances and stand up during the show to proclaim that he knew how to do all of Pinetti's tricks. Pinetti managed to give the impression that this vulgar character was Decremps without actually saying so, quieted the crowd, who resented this intrusion on the entertainment, and gave a few coins to the poor man to go away.

Decremps went on, however, to write other books on conjuring and grew increasingly caustic in his references to Pinetti. This competition and exposure forced Pinetti to invent new material; and the books of Decremps aroused interest in conjuring and brought many new performers to the field of conjuring, both amateur and professional.

Robert - Houdin

LA MAGIE BLANCHE DEVOILÉE and the subsequent books by Decremps were instrumental in creating the first great scientific conjuror. A young watchmaker's apprentice named Jean-Eugene Robert went to a book shop in the early part of the nineteenth century and asked to purchase a treatise on clockmaking. The bookseller accidentally gave him the wrong books; and when Robert reached home, he found that he had several volumes of an encyclopedia on scientific conjuring. He was so fascinated by what he read that he stayed up reading the books until his candle burned out. And then he stole out of the house determined to find another lamp even if he had to steal a street lamp.

Robert had a very logical and imaginative mind. He quickly realized that the books he had read told him how magic was done, but did not teach him to do it. He saw that it was essential to be able to do the secret manipulations required without giving the least hint to the spectators that anything deceptive was being done. To develop skill with his hands he took up practicing juggling. To develop the ability to do secret manipulations while apparently doing something else, he practiced juggling while he read a book or performed other tasks. He took up the practice of card sleight of hand, not only in his non-working hours, but while he was at work, and even when he was at dinner. Men's clothing at the time fortunately included large pockets, and Robert would practice card sleights while he was walking down the street on an errand, or at dinner, by keeping one hand in a pocket. This method of practice gave him the ability to do sleight of hand, while apparently going about ordinary day-to-day affairs in the presence of other people.

Some performers who have practiced too long in front of a mirror never learn to hide the fact that they are doing sleight of hand. There is the danger when practicing in front of a mirror, with yourself as the only audience, to hide the sleights by blinking your eyes or looking in the wrong place at the right time. No performer can count on an audience doing this. On the other hand, practicing in front of an audience is not only damaging to one's morale, but is also damaging to the art of conjuring. Robert's method of practice worked well for him, but it is not so easy with modern clothing. It is possible, however, to practice sleight of hand while reading or watching television and gain some of the benefit of learning to do the secret moves without needing to think about them.

Young Robert went on to marry a girl named Houdin, and in accordance with French custom of the time, changed his name to Jean-Eugene Robert-Houdin. He became the greatest conjurer of his time, and is still revered as the father of modern conjuring.

Before Robert-Houdin's time, conjuring was proceeding along in the tradition of Mediaeval times. One French conjurer, Philippe, even reverted to the costume of the wizards and wore a pointed hat and long robe, in the manner of the ancient alchemists. Bartolomeo Bosco performed the cups and balls much as the trick had been performed in the market places of the villages in the Middle Ages. Robertson, a Belgian optician used mirrors and lenses to produce apparent ghosts, much as the charlatans and black magicians had done long before.

Many conjurers of the period cluttered their stages with great quantities of equipment, little of which was used in the performance. The idea was that the audience would come back and pay another admission for another night in the hope of seeing some of the tricks that were displayed but not shown on the first occasion. Eccentric costumes were the fad among conjurers. Some conjurers were so far behind the times they used tables with long drapes reaching to the floor to conceal an assistant underneath. The assistant was of great help to the magician, who could place an empty container on the table and have it loaded by the assistant, or could have articles exchanged on the table. The device was useful, but not very deceptive.

Robert-Houdin changed all this. He used a simple stage setting with elegant, thin topped tables. He dressed in the same manner as any gentleman would to attend the affair at which he performed. He used no accomplices in the audience. He arranged his stage lighting to concentrate attention on the trick he was performing. His apparatus was simple and unostentatious, and used transparent glass wherever possible to keep the audience from suspecting that there was deception in the properties used. He wrote in his memoirs that real conjuring must be done by the artist, and not by a tinsmith.

Most important of all, he spoke and acted like the cultured gentleman he was. He disdained puns and vulgar humor. He completely divorced charlatanry from conjuring, and when he attributed magical effects to spirits or devils, everyone knew he was not being serious, but was providing an amusing setting for the trick. Having had a good education and having studied watchmaking and the making of automata and complex machines, he was able to introduce spoofing scientific explanations for effects he created. Previously magicians had attributed their powers to familiar spirits or other mysterious agencies. In Robert-Houdin's time, however, the belief in spirits was fading away and the belief in the mysterious powers of science was taking its place.

Robert-Houdin took advantage of this in such tricks as the suspension of his son in mid-air. The anesthetic properties of ether had only recently been discovered, and were not well understood by the general public. To provide some explanation to occupy the mind of the audience and to draw attention away from the fact that his son's elbow rested on a support attached to a steel frame concealed under the boy's clothing, Houdin prefaced the suspension with a scene in which he apparently rendered the boy unconscious with ether. To make this more convincing, he had an off-stage assistant pour a few drops of ether on a hot plate. This was so effective that some people actually wrote vehement protests to Houdin, complaining that he was

Magician catching bird, shot from cannon, on end of sword.
Note variety of apparatus in background (Paris 1852).

Robert Houdin suspends his son in air.

endangering his son's health by subjecting him to this complete loss of weight by the use of a powerful chemical.

Robert-Houdin also used his scientific and mechanical talents to build various automata, which he exhibited in his performances and at scientific exhibitions. Some of these were real automata; they were self-contained and operated by clockwork in the body of the machine. Others were false automata, operated by a human being concealed inside, or else by someone offstage using special built-in mechanisms.

The most celebrated real automaton built by Robert-Houdin was a writing and drawing figure, which won a gold medal in a Paris exposition. It was later sold to the great American showman P.T. Barnum, who exhibited it until it was destroyed in a fire in New York. The figure was of a man dressed in Louis XV style, seated at a small writing table. The face was modeled by Robert-Houdin to look like himself. The automaton was an extremely complicated piece of machinery, capable of drawing various figures, including a greyhound and a cupid, writing Robert-Houdin's signature, and writing down the time of day in response to the control of an internal clock.

Figures such as these had long existed, but were especially popular during the late eighteenth and early nineteenth centuries. In an era when mass production of accurate mechanisms was not even dreamed of, such marvels seemed truly magical. Few of Robert-Houdin's automata have survived, but a figure similar to his writing and drawing figure may still be seen in the Franklin Institute Museum in Philadelphia. This figure was built by a man named Maillardet. It was in ruins when it was acquired by the Museum and no one knew at the time which of the famous writing automata it was. When rebuilt, however, the first thing the figure wrote was a poem signed "written by the automaton of Maillardet."

Robert-Houdin discovered after a time that his automata were so perfect most people were not impressed with their performance. He overheard people say, "Oh it is very clever, but all these things are really very simple when you know how they work." His gardener even said he understood all these complicated machines because he had often greased the weathervane on the roof of the barn.

As a result, Robert-Houdin resolved to exhibit automata that would not only do difficult things, but would do absolutely impossible things. He constructed, for example, an automaton called "The Pastry Cook of the Palais Royal" that consisted of a small figure outside a small building decorated as a pastry shop. The figure would go into the building and return with whatever type of pastry was requested by the audience. It would even accept coins from members of the audience, go into the shop and return with the correct change. Robert-Houdin would borrow a ring from a member of the audience, vanish it, and the little pastry cook figure would go into his shop and return with a small cake, which had the ring baked inside.

How was the machine able to do all this? Houdin was familiar with the famous chess-playing machine of Von Kempelen, later acquired by a man named Maelzel. This machine, which was the subject of stories by Edgar Allan Poe and Ambrose Bierce, was apparently a machine constructed of springs and gears and cams that could play chess against a human opponent and usually win. It was built in 1738 and was still being operated in Atlantic City, New Jersey, in the 1930's. The problem of playing chess is too complex even for a modern computer, but Von Kempelen's machine managed to play very good chess as long as a good human chess player could be employed, for the machine was a fake. The real, human, chess player was cleverly concealed in the machine.

Robert-Houdin's Pastry Cook worked in much the same way. A small boy was concealed, sitting Hindu fashion in the pastry shop; his legs were in the supporting platform. It was he who operated the machine. This of course made the machine a fraud, but it was a permissible fraud since it was presented as a conjuring trick. And after all, no machine even a computer does anything except through the intelligence and skill of a human. In Robert-Houdin's automaton the programmer was simply in continuous and direct control of the work of the machine.

Robert-Houdin's inventiveness, charm, and ability at conjuring soon won him large and enthusiastic audiences. His style of conjuring has influenced the art to the present day. He believed that a conjurer should perform as a gentleman, not as a strangely dressed mountebank. He believed that conjuring apparatus should look elegant but simple. He believed that a conjurer should develop great manual skill, but should not demonstrate that skill directly, but rather use it as one of the means of deception. He believed in creating an interesting and at least momentarily believable atmosphere for each trick.

His success was so great that he was able to retire on a comfortable income (something few conjurers have achieved) and live at Saint Gervais as a country gentleman. The Theatre he had founded continued to be successful for many years in Paris, and one of its later managers and performers became one of the pioneers of the motion picture industry. Georges Melies, conjurer and showman, invented most of the trick photography used in motion pictures to this day.

Robert-Houdin himself was called from retirement by the French government to suppress a revolt in Algeria, which he did by showing the Algerians that French magic was superior to the pretended real magic of their Marabouts. Other than this he devoted his retirement to writing his autobiography, two text-books on conjuring, and a book exposing card sharpers. He also did research on opthalmology, invented electrical devices, and made his home the most scientific household of its time.

He installed clocks operated by electricity in the various buildings on his estate, controlled by a master clock in his study. He installed an automatic feeding system for his horse, controlled in part by the barn door, which had to be locked from the outside before the automatic trough would deliver food to the horse. This prevented the groom from pilfering the grain. He installed a burglar alarm system and an automatic warning system on the gate to the estate. This system was ingeniously arranged to count the number of people who entered and also tell whether each person was a stranger or someone who was accustomed to operating the mechanism. He installed a large clock in the tower of the house and connected the winding mechanism to the swinging door of the kitchen. Thus the servants wound the clock as they went back and forth through the door, without realizing that they were doing any extra work. He invented a remote-reading thermoelectric temperature indicator for his greenhouse so that without going near the place he could amaze the gardener by telling him how well he was maintaining the correct temperature.

Many of Robert-Houdin's creations, including an electric clock made a hundred years ago, are still on exhibit in the technical museum in Paris. His auto-biography remains one of the greatest books ever written by a conjurer, although its accuracy has been questioned. He was a very talented and fortunate man, for he not only found joy in creating and in-venting, but he was able to convey some of that joy to audiences through his skill at performing. He showed that science and art need not be separated.

Maskelyne and Devant

MEANWHILE, across the channel in England, conjuring was thriving equally well; there it was an old and respected art. The English have always been noted for their ability to see, hear, say, and do the most outrageous things without losing either their assurance or their dignity. Possibly for this reason, England has always been very hospitable to conjurers.

During the Middle Ages in England, as in the rest of the world, conjurers who performed simple effects wandered from place to place and performed at fairs and other places where the public might gather. Eventually they began to rent rooms in the part of London which is still its theater district, advertise their performances, and perform in their own small theaters. One sleight of hand performer named Fawkes was able in this way to accumulate a fortune of over fifty thousand dollars in the early part of the eighteenth century.

One of the greatest conjurers of nineteenth century Britain was a Scot, John Henry Anderson, who first

61

proved that conjuring entertainments could fill the largest theaters if the conjurer were a good enough advertiser. Using advertising methods similar to those of a circus, he achieved enough fame to play such famous theaters as Sadler's Wells, and Covent Garden.

Because he came from Scotland, Anderson was known in England as the Wizard of the North, a title that caused him some trouble when he toured the American South during the Civil War period. He claimed the title had been given to him by Sir Walter Scott, and he sometimes had twenty-four men carry three foot high letters spelling out "The Great Wizard of the North" through the streets of London.

For the presentation of conjuring, particularly for large and spectacular effects, it is desirable to have a theater devoted entirely to conjuring. This enables the conjurer to design and build his effects to suit the exact conditions under which they will be presented. Anderson tried several times to build his own theater but was always frustrated by fires and by bank failures and other financial crises.

The most famous theater to be used entirely for conjuring was a small establishment in London known as Egyptian Hall. This was a building constructed with a facade representing the English idea of an Egyptian Temple; it was originally intended as a natural history museum. Built in 1812, its career as a museum lasted only until 1819. From that time on it was used as a theater and exhibition hall, presenting a fantastic variety of attractions from art exhibitions to P.T. Barnum's midget Tom Thumb. In 1865, a conjurer named Colonel Stodare exhibited an illusion there and was so successful that from that time until the hall was torn down in 1905 it continued to present the best in conjuring to the public. Colonel Stodare's illusion was called the "Sphinx," it appeared to be a living head in a box on a table. Although obviously having no body, the head would move and speak when questions were asked of it. Actually, the body was concealed by two forty-five degree mirrors that reflected the sides of the stage set, made of the same material as the background, and gave the illusion that there was nothing under the table. This illusion is well known today, but it startled the public and secured great publicity when it was first introduced.

Colonel Stodare was too good a conjurer to merely exhibit a bodyless head on a table. A further effect was obtained by closing the box, carrying it down to the audience, and speaking to the head in the box, which answered him, though the voice grew fainter and fainter and finally faded away. Thereupon he opened the box and showed that it contained nothing but ashes. This part of the effect he accomplished with ventriloquism.

After Colonel Stodare, many other magicians performed at the hall. Because the theater of the Egyptian Hall was used only by conjurers, it was possible to present many large illusions there that would have been difficult to carry about from place to place.

One illusion that travels with difficulty and was often done at Egyptian Hall is known as "Pepper's Ghost." This was invented by a Professor Pepper of the London Polytechnic Institute and requires a very large sheet of plate glass. If you look out the window of your house during the day you see the outdoors very clearly. If you look out at night, however, when it is dark outside and the room is illuminated, you will see a reflection of the room you are in. This is the principle of Pepper's illusion. A large sheet of plate glass is set at an angle on stage and the scene behind the glass is brightly illuminated. The ghost is located where it cannot be seen by the audience directly but would be seen reflected on the glass if the glass were a mirror. Then the lights on the scene are dimmed, and the ghost is brightly illuminated. This causes the reflection of the ghost to be seen in the glass, superimposed on the scene without the glass itself being seen. It is a beautiful illusion, but the glass is difficult to transport.

Eventually John Nevil Maskelyne, one of the greatest of English conjurers, took over Egyptian Hall and operated it for thirty-one years, until he moved to a new theater of conjuring at St. Georges Hall. Maskelyne performed in the theater himself and also presented other conjurers there. Maskelyne was a man of many talents ranging from watchmaking to juggling. Like Robert-Houdin he was a man with a scientific mind. He not only invented conjuring devices and presentations, but he did research on high speed photography, invented coin-operated devices, and did research on the filling of balloons.

Because of Maskelyne's interest in mechanical things, many of his illusions were mechanical devices rather than sleight of hand. He built many automata including a figure mounted on a glass column, and thus isolated from the stage, which could play a game of whist with a spectator, perform mathematical calculations, and even play chess. This time there was no chance of an assistant concealed in the works,

The automation of Maskelyne—
front and back.

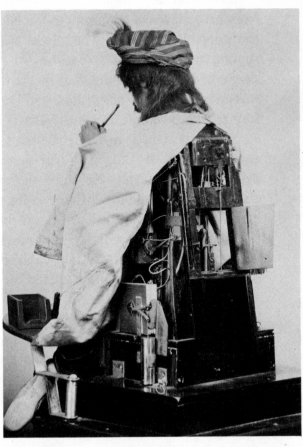

since the figure was much too small to conceal a human and was held up from the stage by a transparent glass column. Many explanations were offered as to how the trick was worked, ranging from compressed air to the rotation of a second glass column inside the visible supporting column. But Maskelyne and his son and grandson declined to verify any of the explanations, and if you want to figure it out, you will have to go to the Kensington Museum in London where the figure is still on exhibition. But you will be none the wiser after your visit, for not even the staff of the museum knows how the figure was operated.

Maskelyne later joined forces with David Devant, one of the cleverest conjurers in the history of English conjuring. Devant, like Maskelyne, was clever at inventing new deceptions, but he was more able in sleight of hand and acting than his partner. Maskelyne was an inventor who performed, and Devant was a performer who invented. Devant charmed audiences with conjuring designed to be something more than a demonstration of skill with the hands or skill in designing mechanisms. He acted the part of a magician by giving some sort of plot to his effects. For example, when he vanished a girl on the stage he did not simply cover her with a cloth and then fire a pistol and quickly show that she had vanished. Devant had a girl costumed for a moth dance on stage, and he endeavored to attract her to the flame of a candle, which he carried as he pantomimed temptation. When she finally came near him, he reached for her and she seemed to dissolve into nothingness and vanish completely, leaving him alone on stage.

In addition to his original inventions, Devant performed many tricks that had been invented by others but he always used his originality to provide a new setting, and a plot as well as combining various elements to make a new overall creation.

Maskelyne's theater had no rival except the little theater in Paris founded by Robert-Houdin, which perished before Maskelyne's when it was torn down to widen a boulevard. Maskelyne's theater lasted until, after a disagreement among John Nevil's grandsons, it was purchased by the BBC to be used as a television studio.

Herrmann, Hoffmann, and Buatier

IF THERE WAS one weakness in Robert-Houdin's style of conjuring, it was the lack of a distinctive character. He was too much the gentleman conjurer to serve as the image of a magician in the public mind. His magic was more for the mind than for the emotions.

The man who was destined to create the type of character conjurers would play for many years to come was born in France, of German parents, went to school in Austria, and later became a citizen of the United States. His name was Alexander Herrmann. There are few people now living who saw him perform, for he died in 1896, but there is probably no one living who has not seen a conjurer imitate the style created by Herrmann. Anyone who has ever seen a cartoon, painting, photograph, or live performer wearing a mustache and goatee, pulling a rabbit from a hat, and smiling impishly at the audience, has seen the character created by Alexander Herrmann.

Herrmann played the part of a friendly, humorous, lovable devil. He was not a great innovator in conjuring, but he was possibly its greatest natural performer. He constantly played the part he had created, on stage and off. He often told people that conjurers were born and not made, and it is possible that in his case this was true. Just as some people are natural comedians and cannot say anything without it having a comic effect on other people, Herrmann was a natural conjurer. He could no more stop amazing people than he could stop eating.

Herrmann had superbly skillful hands, but even more important he had the ability to be one jump ahead of his audience psychologically. Because of this, he could afford to be one of the most audacious conjurers ever known. He would, for example, walk into the audience and produce fish bowls full of water and goldfish from a borrowed handkerchief, while surrounded by spectators. He once plucked a bundle of cigars from the beard of President U.S. Grant.

Herrmann was always ready to perform miracles. At a dinner he would raise his wine glass in a toast, then throw the glass into the air where the glass and the wine in it would seem to disappear in mid-air. People might have thought that Herrmann dropped the glass into his lap in the action of throwing it into the air. But Herrmann's sense of artistic completeness was greater than that. Shortly after the vanish, he would get up from the table and walk away. If anyone thought that he had left the glass on the chair or anywhere else, he would find that there was no glass to be found and there was no evidence that Herrmann was concealing the full glass of wine on his person.

On stage Herrmann performed magic ranging from pure sleight of hand to the largest illusions, as large mechanical tricks are called. In most cases he took material invented by others and dramatized it to make it real magic for an audience. Creativity in conjuring has always had two facets: creativity in devising methods, and creativity in devising presentation. Very few individuals have been great in both.

Herrmann performed the second sight act devised by Pinetti and improved by Robert-Houdin. He performed the decapitation that had been described by Reginald Scot. He performed the vanishing bird cage and the vanishing lady invented by Buatier de Kolta, a French magician who was very inventive but not the greatest of performers. He performed a bullet catching trick, which had been invented by an English riding master to protect participants in a duel from being hurt. To all these, Herrmann brought his own special magic, the magic of superb acting skill. Herrmann did not invent many new illusions, but neither did Paganini invent the violin.

While Herrmann was advancing the art of presentation, an English lawyer, Angelo Lewis, was advancing its technical level. An amateur conjurer himself, he felt that conjuring was depending too much on traditional technical methods. So he wrote a book on conjuring that told everyone exactly how most of the tricks then being done were accomplished, hoping that this would stimulate the invention of new methods. For his book he leaned rather heavily on the work of J.N. Ponsin, a Frenchman whose book on conjuring updated the works of Decremps. Fearing that his law clients would not trust an expert in the art of deception, he had the book published under the pen name of Professor Hoffmann.

Portrait of
Buatier deKolta

Herrmann the Great catching Krag-Jorgensen rifle bullets
fired by soldiers at the Baldwin Theatre, San Francisco.

This book was more successful than any other work ever published on the subject of conjuring. Its title is *Modern Magic,* and it may still be purchased in conjuring shops. Its author went on to write three sequels: *More Magic, Later Magic,* and *Latest Magic.* He also translated the works of Robert-Houdin into English, wrote a novel about a conjurer and a play that employed conjuring as its main device, and produced many other works on conjuring, puzzles, parlor games, and scientific amusements. He became the foremost authority on conjuring, although he was not much of a performer himself and did not invent much that was new in conjuring.

The tricks he was writing about, and Herrmann was producing, some of them at least, were being invented by a man named Joseph Buatier in France. Joseph Buatier was an eccentric man even in an eccentric profession. Born in Caluire et Cuire, near Lyon, France, he was expected by his family to enter the priesthood. Instead he added his mother's maiden name to his own last name and became Buatier de Kolta, the conjurer. During his entire career he never bought a piece of conjuring equipment. With a set of tools consisting of little more than a screwdriver, pliers, awl, wire cutters, knife and a file he constructed equipment of his own design that astounded the world of conjuring.

Buatier looked very little like Mephistopheles. He looked more like an ill-kept U.S. Grant, with a full beard, high collar, long velvet coat and tight but wrinkled pants. He was concerned almost entirely with the illusionary effect of his creations and not at all with beautiful stage decor and elaborate costumes. He performed on a bare stage, although even here he had one idiosyncrasy: he insisted that a bare floor was unattractive and always had a carpet on the stage.

His inventions are still being used by conjurers all over the world, for he invented the vanishing bird cage, the multiplying billiard balls, the production of spring flowers from a paper cone, the vanish of a lady from a chair, and was probably the inventor of the Black Art act.

Buatier's vanish of a lady from a chair was considered by Alexander Herrmann to be the greatest stage trick ever invented. Buatier would spread a newspaper on the stage, to prevent suspicion of a stage trapdoor, place a chair on the newspaper and then have his lady assistant sit in the chair. He covered the lady with a cloth for a moment, then whisked away the cloth and both it and the lady disappeared, leaving only the chair and the newspaper. Despite appearances, the lady vanished through a trapdoor. The stage floor, the carpet, and the newspaper were all provided with traps, and the seat of the chair folded down to allow the lady to slide through the traps and below the stage. The time of her disappearance was concealed by having thin wire forms extend from the chair to simulate her form under the cloth. The cloth vanished under Buatier's coat by means of an elastic pull.

Buatier's last and possibly greatest illusion was an eight-inch cube painted to look like a die, which suddenly expanded to sixty-four times its original volume. Buatier brought the eight-inch cube on stage in a satchel early in his performance, telling the audience that his wife was in the satchel. He built up the effect by telling the assistants not to trip over the satchel during the show, because they might injure his wife. For his final trick, he removed the die from the satchel and placed it on a table. Suddenly the cube expanded, he walked over to it, lifted it and revealed his wife, who had apparently been in it.

Buatier was a great inventor and technician but a poor showman. Because of this he had little financial success. When friends urged him to improve his showmanship, he said that it didn't matter. If a man achieved what he set out to achieve, he was happy. Buatier achieved a great deal, for his inventions were used by many others to entertain untold millions of people.

Kellar and Thurston

A WHOLE generation of conjurers grew up inspired by the great Herrmann, instructed by Professor Hoffmann, and thrilled by Buatier's tricks, done by others. In 1876 a young boy named Howard Thurston witnessed a performance by Herrmann and was so impressed that he resolved to some day become a magician. A few years later he found a copy of *Modern Magic* in a second-hand book store and, like many other boys, started practicing sleight of hand during his every spare moment. The love of conjuring was the one constant factor in his life from that time on.

Thurston flailed about wildly in attempts to find his place in the world. He had a love of adventure that drove him away from home and into selling programs at race tracks to earn a living. He followed carnivals from town to town and associated with con men, race-track touts and criminals. He was a school dropout and a juvenile delinquent. But under all this was a deep moral sense that eventually compelled him to stop wasting his life and study for the ministry. He studied hard and was leaving to begin a career as a missionary when once again he saw Alexander Herrmann. In all the years since he had first seen Herrmann, Thurston had continued to practice conjuring. After the performance, something close to real magic happened when Thurston went to buy a train ticket to Philadelphia, where he was to receive his final training as a medical missionary. At the station Herrmann was standing in front of him in the ticket line. Herrmann asked for a ticket to Syracuse, and when Thurston asked for a ticket to Philadelphia, he was accidentally given one to Syracuse. The ticket agent's error converted the missionary to conjuring. Thurston followed Herrmann to Syracuse, watched him perform again, and decided to become a professional conjurer.

He returned home, practiced sleight of hand all that winter and then set out as a conjurer, obtaining his first job in a carnival. His skill and his professional status advanced steadily until he became the foremost conjurer of his time. His adventurous boyhood had taught him to be resourceful and audacious, and his training under the great evangelist Dwight L. Moody had taught him the art of public speaking. He also had great skill with his hands and possessed the indefinable quality of all great performers that enables them to command attention just by appearing in public.

In the early part of the twentieth century vaudeville was one of the most popular forms of entertainment. Because of his great skill at card sleight of hand, Thurston became the first person to present a full vaudeville act using only a deck of cards. As a finish he did produce a duck from the coat of someone in the audience, but basically his entire act was done with a deck of cards. Using a sleight that was probably the creation of a forgotten Mexican gambler, Thurston vanished cards into thin air one by one, then reproduced them one by one, showing his hands empty all during the process. Specific cards called for by the audience would rise mysteriously from a deck in his hand up to his other hand, held above the pack. He could throw playing cards into the hands of members of the audience, even when they were seated in the highest balcony of the largest theater. He proved that tricks with cards were not restricted to small groups of people at a card table or in a living room.

Alexander Herrmann had died before Thurston achieved international fame, but his nephew Leon, who looked very much like his uncle but lacked his theatrical flair, had carried on the show. With the assistance of Leon Herrmann's stage manager, Thurston performed his rising card trick for the nephew of the great Herrmann, and succeeded in fooling him completely. From that day on Thurston was known as "The man who fooled Herrmann."

Aided by this publicity, Thurston gradually built up his show until it became a spectacular stage offering, with assistants dressed as oriental dancing girls and Nubian slaves. He continued to feature his skill with playing cards, but also made his girl assistants vanish, caused a golden ball to float in the air, materialized a statue that visibly changed to a living girl, produced inflated balloons from an empty opera hat, and produced fountains of water from nowhere.

Thurston toured the world with great success until he was called back to the United States to take over the show of another great American magician, Harry Kellar, who had decided to retire from the theater.

Harry Kellar, although a contemporary of Alexander Herrmann, had an entirely different style of performance. Herrmann was dashing, debonair, and continental. He was brilliant at improvisation and could handle any emergency that arose during a performance. Kellar was much more deliberate and mysterious. He did not need to be good at improvisation because he was so much a perfectionist that emergencies just did not happen when he was performing.

One of Kellar's tricks involved the vanishing of a lamp from a glass-topped table. The trick itself was mysterious enough, for the light from the lamp could be seen after the lamp was covered with a foulard and the glass lamp chimney could be seen projecting above the foulard. When Kellar fired a pistol the light went out, the foulard fell to the table, and the lamp seemed to melt away into nothingness. Many magicians would have performed this trick silently, others would have used humorous comments to enliven it; but Kellar made it more impressive by telling the audience that the lamp had been given to him by a Brahmin holy man from Benares, India on condition that he return it to the Brahmin by magic at a certain hour each evening. At this point a bell would strike the hour slowly and mysteriously, and Kellar would cover the lamp with the foulard explaining that when he fired a pistol, the atoms of the lamp would be converted into the fourth dimension and fly to Benares where they would be reassembled into the same lamp.

This style of conjuring performance is not easy. The execution of the trick must be flawless, and the performer's acting skill must keep the audience under con-

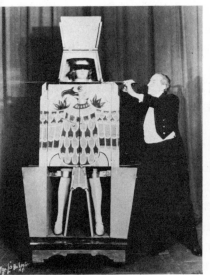 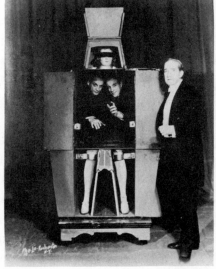

Thurston creates the bodyless woman.

trol and make them believe for the moment that they are seeing a miracle. It is much safer for a conjurer to do comedy, for then anything that goes wrong can be covered up by more comedy. Thurston was able to create the same atmosphere of mystery after he took over Kellar's show. Thurston was aided in this by his impressive bearing, his great skill in speaking, and by the fact that he had traveled all over the world before he was appointed by Kellar as his successor. It gave him the necessary prestige.

Although difficult to achieve, the Kellar-Thurston style of almost-serious dramatic presentation is probably the highest form of conjuring. For example, Kellar developed and Thurston improved an illusion involving the levitation of a young lady assistant. In Thurston's presentation of the illusion, he would announce to the audience, after causing the girl to float from a couch into the air and out over the orchestra pit, that he would show them something they would never forget as long as they lived. He then whisked away the cloth that had been covering the girl, and she vanished in mid-air. He was absolutely correct. No one who saw this act ever forgot.

The difficulty of maintaining this atmosphere of genuine mystery was illustrated when Thurston died and his show was carried on for a time by a much younger performer. Although a very clever magician in his own way, the younger man was never able to impress the public in the way Thurston had. Audiences saw him as a clever young man who did tricks, not as a dignified, though often humorous, gentleman who could perform miracles.

Houdini Escapes

IN ADDITION to being a master of the presentation of large illusions, Kellar was very active in exposing the tricks of fraudulent spirit mediums. He performed their tricks and told his audience that they were done by perfectly natural, scientific, and non-supernatural means. He was too good a showman to expose all the methods he used in reproducing spiritualistic phenomena to the public, but he convinced most audiences that what he said was true.

Kellar had more knowledge of fake mediums than most conjurers because early in his career he had been assistant and business manager to two of the greatest fake mediums who ever lived. They were the Davenport brothers, who produced spirit phenomena while they were securely tied to seats in a small cabinet. Musical instruments were placed in the cabinet with them and, after the men were tied by the audience and the doors to the cabinet were closed, the instruments would be heard playing. Sometimes the instruments were thrown out of the cabinet as though by some spirit force. A spectator would sometimes be invited into the cabinet with the tied brothers. As soon as the doors were closed, the audience would hear a commotion and the spectator would rush out of the cabinet with his jacket coat turned inside out. The brothers were still securely tied, and it did not seem possible that they had had anything to do with the mysterious events. Sometimes they even let the audience put flour in their hands before the doors were closed. After the spirit manifestations, the doors would be opened and the brothers would still be securely tied, the flour still in their hands, with no evidence of flour spilled in the cabinet, as would have been the case had they released themselves.

The Davenport brothers were accepted by many as genuine mediums, and they presented their performance seriously. But they were ultimately exposed as tricksters. Their exposers ranged from Robert-Houdin to a group of college students who lit matches at a prearranged signal, thereby exposing the brothers running around, when they were supposed to be in their cabinet securely tied down to the seats. More than one amateur magician became a professional after seeing how thoroughly the Davenports fooled audiences with relatively simple rope tying tricks.

How did the Davenports escape from the ropes that bound them? By means of a trick rope tie that their father had learned from the American Indians who used it in their religious ceremonies. The father taught it to his two sons. Kellar learned it from them and presented it as part of his entertainment. And a boy named Ehrich Weiss saw Kellar perform the rope escape and was fascinated. Later the boy was to borrow Kellar's first name and the last name of Robert-Houdin and set out to become the greatest escape artist of all time—Harry Houdini.

Like many geniuses, Harry Houdini was a man of many conflicts and contradictions. The son of an educated and cultured man, he rejected scholarship and even the essentials of grammar. Although deeply attached to his mother, he became a wanderer and performed all over the world. His boyhood idol was Robert-Houdin, but when he had become the Great Houdini he was snubbed by a relative of Robert-Houdin and thereupon wrote a book that tried to prove Robert-Houdin was a fraud. His ambition was to become a debonair and suave magician like Robert-Houdin and Alexander Herrmann, but instead he became famous for his challenge escapes, which he considered publicity for his real show.

When his mother died, he became sincerely interested in spiritualism; but he was too expert in the art of deception to be fooled by fraudulent spirit mediums. He therefore became the foremost enemy of spiritualism and exposed its fakery in his performances. He was the most arrogant of men, but he was also the most gentle and the most generous. He defied the world to outwit him, and he won. He played the part of a superman for so long that he came to believe it himself. And in a way he was right. He was no ordinary man.

As a straight conjurer, Houdini was ordinary. He became an extraordinary performer when he developed a style of performance in which he challenged the audience to a battle, fought them and won. He defied anyone to tie him, handcuff him, or imprison him so that he could not escape. His technical skill was so great that he almost invariably won; his few failures were minor and not well publicized. He escaped from rope ties, handcuffs, strait jackets, bank vaults, milk cans, a water torture cell, a Siberian prison van, jail cells, glass boxes, mail pouches, roll top desks, boilers, coffins, and even from a paper bag without damaging the bag.

Even when he performed straight conjuring, Houdini was most successful with feats that contained some element of challenge. One of his most famous tricks was swallowing a number of needles and a piece of thread. He would show his mouth empty and then draw the thread from his mouth with the needles strung on the thread. He used the challenge technique by inviting a committee up from the audience to inspect his mouth during the progress of the trick, even specifying that he would prefer to have a committee of doctors.

All during his career, Houdini used for his formal performances an illusion known as the Substitution Trunk. The performer or his assistant is handcuffed, placed in a sack, and is then locked in a trunk. The trunk is tied securely with ropes on all sides, and the assistant or performer, whichever was not placed in the trunk, holds a cloth in front of him or her up to the neck then counts 1-2—. At the count of 2 the cloth is raised and immediately dropped as the one who was in the trunk says 3. The individual in the trunk has changed places with the one who was holding the cloth and standing on top of the trunk. This is verified, of course, by untying the trunk, unlocking it and opening the sack to find the person who a moment before was standing on the trunk in full view. This

Houdini
suspended upside-down in a
variety of strait jacket.

Houdini among his books

trick depends for much of its effect on the speed with which the exchange is made. Houdini challenged the world to produce someone who could do the trick as fast as it was performed by him and his wife. Always in his presentation there was this element of challenge.

Houdini's style of performance, a mixture of challenge, dynamic personality, and charm, is as dangerous for the average performer as the serious and mysterious style of Kellar. It has often been attempted by performers who found that their audiences rose all too well to the challenge. Houdini succeeded with it because he was an extraordinary man. If he had been an artist, he would have been Leonardo da Vinci; if he had been a politician, he would have been Disraeli. His field however was in entertaining people by playing the part of the superman almost everyone would like to be. He was the one and only Houdini.

Robinson as Chung Ling Soo

OCCASIONALLY conjuring has produced an all around talent who can invent, produce, assist, work out effective theatrical presentations, do sleight of hand, and possesses the acting technique and publicity sense to create a public character that attracts enormous attention.

William E. Robinson was such a man although he was nearly forty years old before he found a format in which he could effectively use all his skill. Robinson was trained as a metal worker, but his real interest was in conjuring and while still a young man he toured as "Robinson, the man of mystery." It was a prophetic title for all through his life Robinson was a man of mystery both in conjuring and in private life.

Early in his career Robinson married a dancer named Olive Path, later known as Dot because of her small size, and began performing what is known as a Black Art magic act. This act, which was probably invented by Buatier, creates its illusions by hiding black covered objects in front of a black background. If the lighting is arranged properly even an assistant clothed in black is invisible before the black background and may move about the stage unseen by the audience. To cause an object to appear, the assistant can remove the black cover from the object. To vanish it, he can cover it with black cloth. To cause it to float in the air, he merely lifts it, being careful not to put his hands where they will show against the light-colored object. The principle has often been used in recent years in motion pictures and on television for dance acts, puppets, and trick photography for commercials.

While performing this act under the name of Achmed ben Ali, Robinson was hired by Harry Kellar as his chief assistant and illusion builder. Robinson designed and built many of Kellar's greatest illusions, and Robinson, using the name Nana Sahib, and his wife were among the greatest conjurer's assistants ever known. They were especially valuable to Kellar in his exposés of fake spiritualism, for Robinson had one of the best informed, as well as one of the most inventive minds, in conjuring. His extensive collection of books on conjuring eventually became the nucleus of the present New York Public Library collection of books on the subject.

Changing his name again, this time to Abdul Khan, Robinson left Kellar and went to work for Alexander Herrmann as chief assistant and illusion builder. Sometime between the jobs for Kellar and Herrmann, Robinson operated a book shop under the name of Campbell. During this period he invented an illusion used by both Kellar and Herrmann. It was called "Gone" and involved the disappearance of a girl from a chair that had been hoisted into the air by ropes. At a signal from the conjurer, the girl would disappear in mid-air while the pieces of the chair fell to the floor. The chair was made in sections, held together by the girl, and a piece of plate glass was built into the supporting frame for the ropes. After the girl had been hoisted up behind the plate glass, the lighting was suddenly changed, as in the "Pepper's ghost" illusion, the girl released the pieces of the chair, which dropped to the stage, and she remained supported by the ropes behind the plate glass, invisible to the audience. Later Robinson modified the illusion to eliminate the problem of transporting the heavy glass and substituted a black cloth for the glass, operating the vanish like the Black Art vanishes.

Robinson's varied talents were so great that Herrmann relied on him not only to build new illusions and effects for his show, and to assist on stage with the entire performance, but sometimes also allowed Robinson to perform as Herrmann. When Herrmann wanted a day off, Robinson would make up as Herrmann and do the entire show without the audience ever knowing that they had not seen Herrmann at all.

After Herrmann's death, Robinson became assistant to Leon Herrmann, the nephew of Alexander, who took over the show. Robinson was the stage manager who helped Thurston fool Leon Herrmann and gave Thurston his first great boost to fame.

Eventually Robinson grew tired of being the invisible genius behind other performers and returned to the stage as "Robinson, the man of mystery." Strangely enough, although he was regarded by other conjurers as a genius, Robinson did not impress the public when he performed as himself. He had trouble getting bookings; so when the foremost Chinese conjurer, Ching Ling Foo, then touring America, offered a thousand dollars to anyone who could duplicate his feats, Robinson quickly worked out methods of duplicating Ching's entire act and accepted the challenge. The offer turned out to be a publicity stunt, and Robinson received nothing from it but the experience of developing and practicing a Chinese conjuring act.

The experience, though, gave Robinson an idea. Why not continue to be the man behind the scenes, but for himself? He would continue to invent and develop, but perform in public as a great Chinese conjurer. He went to Paris and opened in the Folies Bergère as the celebrated Chinese magician Hop Sing Loo. The first performance was a disaster. His equipment failed, and the audience booed him.

But Robinson did not give up easily. His manager suggested that the name Hop Sing Loo sounded more like a laundry than a magician and changed the name to Chung Ling Soo. Robinson did not object, possibly still annoyed with Ching Ling Foo for not paying the thousand dollars.

Opening in England as Chung Ling Soo, Robinson was an instant success. He had finally come into his own, and for the next eighteen years he was one of the greatest attractions in English variety theater. For publicity he pretended to be a real Chinese mandarin and gave press interviews in a dimly lit room to obscure too accurate observations of his American features beneath his makeup. He hired a Chinese acrobat as his interpreter and would answer the reporter's questions in a language of his own invention, which was then translated by the interpreter.

More and more, as time went by, Robinson, the man
of mystery, disappeared behind the mask of his creation Chung Ling Soo. He began to collect Oriental
art objects and rode about London in an elaborate
carriage, an umbrella held over his head by a Chinese
servant.

Eventually Ching Ling Foo, the real Chinese conjurer, brought his show to England and was astounded
to discover that most people regarded him as an im-
itator. This time Robinson challenged Foo to a contest
to see which was the better Chinese miracle worker.
Foo refused on the grounds that Robinson was not
even Chinese, and for a time the London newspapers
published headlines like "Can Soo fool Foo?" and
"Will Foo sue Soo?"

After the dust of this conflict had settled down, Foo
went back to China and Robinson remained the greatest Chinese conjurer in the world. Actually Robinson's Chinese act contained very little real Chinese
conjuring. Most of it consisted of items invented by
Robinson or developed by him from well known
western conjuring principles. All that Robinson borrowed from the Chinese was a character to play. The
things the character did were original with him, although he did them so well that many of them came to
be accepted later as Chinese tricks and the success he
achieved was largely responsible for the emphasis on
Chinese decoration that persists in conjuring to the
present day.

Although the greatest, Robinson was not the only
western conjurer to perform in the disguise of an oriental. Theodore Bamberg, whose family had been conjurers in Holland for six generations, became deaf

before he was twenty and from that time on performed in pantomime as a Chinese magician under the name of Okito. Originally he intended to perform as a Japanese magician and constructed the name Okito by rearranging the letters in Tokio. However Chinese costumes were then more readily obtainable in Amsterdam, so he switched to a Chinese character without changing names.

Both Chung Ling Soo and Okito developed and performed feats that far surpassed anything done by real Chinese conjurers. Authentic Chinese conjuring, although excellent, is limited in scope and done in a fixed, traditional way. It does not take advantage of new technical methods to accomplish new effects.

By pretending ignorance of the language of the audience, both men were able to concentrate on the visual aspect of conjuring, which is the most important. Okito's most famous feat was causing a large sphere to rise from a chest, float in the air, and return to the chest. Described in words this sounds like nothing, but done with Okito's pantomime, lighting, and music, the floating sphere almost made other conjurers in the audience believe in magic.

Robinson, although he did small feats very effectively, was most famous for his large illusions. He fired his wife Dot, now known as Suee Seen, from a cannon, produced her from a cauldron of boiling water, changed her into an orange tree, and produced her from a transparent oriental lantern suspended above the stage. All these effects were produced with great attention to eye appeal. Chung Ling Soo's sets were elaborate, his assistants gorgeously costumed, and his equipment looked like what it was supposed to be.

Blackstone

HARRY BLACKSTONE, possibly the last of the great illusionists in the tradition of Herrmann, Kellar, and
Thurston, was like Herrmann, a natural performer. He
loved conjuring, he loved performing, he loved people,
and he loved life. Most of the feats he performed were
invented by others, but the presentation was all Blackstone.

He was not content to perform the vanishing bird
cage the way its inventor, De Kolta, had. After Blackstone had vanished the cage, he would say, "Give me
a moment to get another cage, and I'll show you that
again." While he went off stage, two showgirls came
on stage and performed a simple conjuring feat, or
a juggling trick. Blackstone came on again and asked
for some children to come up out of the audience.
When they did, he instructed one of them to put his
hands on the top and bottom of the cage, which was
held between Blackstone's palms. Another was told to
put his hands on the front and back of the cage. This
continued until hands surrounded the cage on all sides.

Suddenly Blackstone gave a start and the cage disappeared, mystifying the children on stage as much as the audience.

Unlike Herrmann, Blackstone was not born into a theatrical family. His family name was Bouton, and his father was a hat manufacturer in Chicago. Young Harry saw a performance by Harry Kellar and was fired with the desire to become a conjurer like Kellar. He asked his father how he could learn to do things like Kellar, and his father sent him to the public library where he found Professor Hoffmann's books. He studied and practiced until, seven years later, in 1904, he and his brother Pete set out to entertain the world with an act they called, "Straight and Crooked Magic."

It is almost impossible to create an effective conjuring act when more than one person performs the apparent miracles. Many people can be in the show as assistants, but the focus of attention must be on the one individual who can defy the laws of nature. Miracles that can be performed by many people cease to be miracles. The Bouton Brothers found that their performances were better received if Harry did the performing and Pete served as the backstage technician.

Blackstone eventually began billing himself as Frederick the Great, which proved to be an unfortunate choice of stage names when World War I broke out. He was standing in front of the Blackstone Hotel in Chicago discussing this problem with his agent, and the agent pointed to the marquee. From that time on he was known as Harry Blackstone.

Some performers are spoken of admiringly by other performers as, "magician's magicians." Blackstone was

A typical Blackstone staging.

more than this, he was an audience's magician. With a small mustache, wild hair like Albert Einstein's, and a lively, impish sense of humor, he looked and acted the part of a congenial wizard. He was sometimes referred to as the Ziegfeld of magic because he decorated his stage with beautiful girls in elaborate costumes. The girls were not present merely to stand about on stage and look beautiful, however. He floated them in the air, sawed them in half, produced them from empty cabinets, pushed electric light bulbs through them, and chased one of them into a rack of automobile tires.

Blackstone at work.

When the tires were rolled away one at a time, the girl was nowhere to be found; but when the same tires were stacked vertically, a rope was lowered from above the stage and raised with the girl clinging to it, produced miraculously from the stack of tires.

Blackstone had many talents. He not only fired blank pistols at boxes while beautiful girls appeared and disappeared, he also performed sleight of hand with cards, escapes like those of Houdini, and the rope tie that had been made famous by Kellar.

One of his most charming routines was done with a handkerchief borrowed from someone in the audience. He tied a knot in one corner of the handkerchief, saying, "Now I am going to show you a real live spook." He placed the handkerchief in a cabinet and as the orchestra played weird and unearthly music, the handkerchief could be seen stirring, coming to life, raising itself to look out one of the openings in the cabinet. The handkerchief then climbed out of the cabinet and followed Blackstone across the stage. It even danced with him and insisted on leading rather than following. When he picked it up and took it back into the audience to return it, it kept on moving and squirming in his hand until its owner touched it. Only then did it revert to being a lifeless bit of cloth. The cabinet was by Karl Germain, and the idea of a dancing handkerchief was borrowed from Anna Eva Fay, a famous fake medium. But only a truly great conjurer could have transported audiences into the world of make believe so convincingly using essentially nothing but a handkerchief and a bit of thread.

One of Blackstone's greatest large illusions was the levitation of a girl in full light. This illusion was originally invented by John Nevil Maskelyne, but was improved by Kellar after he retired. Kellar had tried unsuccessfully to buy the trick from Maskelyne and finally became so determined to secure it that he sat in the audience at Egyptian Hall, waited until the levitation was being performed, and simply walked up on stage and looked at the equipment. Maskelyne was so astounded at this un-British conduct that he was speechless. Conjuring equipment is seldom patented because it is not intended for general use and cannot be kept secret and also patented. Anyone can obtain a copy of a patent for a small fee.

Maskelyne originally levitated his partner, Mr. Cooke, and passed a solid hoop completely over him to prove the absence of any support. Kellar and Thurston improved the presentation by pretending to hypnotize a girl and then levitating her, thus providing a false explanation for the levitation much as Robert-Houdin had provided for his earlier and much less technically sophisticated levitation. Blackstone added his own touch by performing the levitation in a harem setting with many showgirls decorating the stage.

Blackstone's career extended almost entirely through the first six decades of the twentieth century. He knew how to survive in the economically dangerous world of live theater. When he and Thurston played the same town at the same time he not only had his advertising posters up first, but he had them coated with lard. When Thurston's bill posters tried to paste their announcements of Thurston's show over Blackstone's, as he had expected they would, the paste failed to stick and Thurston's posters fell to the ground.

When Blackstone began his career, he intended to

do a full evening show as Kellar had. When vaudeville combined with motion pictures became popular, Blackstone put together a superb one hour show and played vaudeville, not as a single act, but as the entire vaudeville unit. When vaudeville showed signs of dying, Blackstone went back to the full show and played in legitimate theaters and civic auditoriums all over the United States and Canada. During World War II he not only made personal appearances at hospitals and army installations but took his entire show with a cast of thirty-eight people to army camps and navy bases.

To be a great conjurer requires talent, personality, endurance, and a passionate love of conjuring. Unlike most actors a conjurer must be on stage and in command of the performance during the entire show. When he is off stage he must be ready to entertain everyone with whom he comes in contact. He must perform for benefits, for the press, for publicity, for local conjurers societies, he must always be a conjurer.

Blackstone was such a great conjurer, and now that he is gone there are, for the first time since Alexander Herrmann, no great conjurers in America. There are specialists in many branches of conjuring who are better in their specialty than Blackstone would have been, but only once in a generation does a conjurer appear who can play the part of a great magician.

The Inventive Geniuses

TODAY MAGIC is changing. Herrmann, Kellar, Robinson and Blackstone used money and all the resources of the theater and all the techniques of advertising to make conjuring a popular form of mass entertainment. Many other conjurers both before and since have done the same thing. But some of the most ingenious and inventive conjurers have been men who have performed without elaborate sets and without scores of assistants, often in halls, studios, drawing rooms, and even in tents. Today, when the theater no longer has a place for elaborate conjuring acts, these performances are most important.

Such performances began years ago. More than a century ago, in Vienna, a Doctor of Philosophy, employed by the Civil Service, constructed his own studio and gave programs of conjuring three times a week. It became fashionable for the elite of the Austrian capital to attend these performances. The man was Dr. Johann Nepomuk Hofsinzer, one of the greatest creative geniuses of all time in the field of conjuring with playing cards. Many of the methods of card conjuring invented by Hofsinzer are still used by conjurers, most of whom do not realize their debt to this man who was famous only in his home city. Hofsinzer showed that apparent miracles could be accomplished with such inexpensive stage properties as cards with faces on both sides or with cards distinguishable by touch because they varied in thickness from the rest of the pack. In addition to being a master of sleight of hand, he was a master of subtlety.

In America at about the same time many conjurers found a fertile field in the lyceum and Chautauqua circuits. These were organized systems for bringing performers, lecturers, and musicians to the thousands of towns and villages before the motion pictures and television. One of the most inventive of these lyceum performers was Charles Mattmueller, of Cleveland Ohio, who performed under the name of Karl Germain. Constantly traveling and performing under all sorts of conditions, he could not carry heavy equipment, sets, or costumes and he never had more than two assistants. He invented, designed, and constructed much of his equipment himself assisted by his father who was an expert wood worker. Some of his equipment was made of laminated paper which he glued, sanded, and painted with great artistry.

Looking like Mephistopheles without a beard, Germain performed such feats as passing a solid wooden board through another solid wooden board; growing a rose bush visibly in an empty flower pot; causing five jars, shown to be empty, to fill suddenly to the brim with water; opening a giant padlock by passing the shadow of its key over the shadow of the lock; and demonstrating mind reading and spirit tricks.

Germain produced the effect of large illusions with a minimum of properties. He would put on an Indian costume and step into an Indian basket on a table, slowly lowering himself into the basket. A man dressed in an overcoat would walk up from the audience, look in the basket, tip it over and show that it was empty. When he removed the overcoat, the man from the audience was seen to be Germain himself. The apparatus for this illusion was easy to carry, the basket was used to pack other equipment when traveling.

Germain also invented an illusion that has been widely used as an advertising window display in stores. The illusion creates the effect of a stream of water continually issuing from a faucet which is suspended by a string and isolated from any source of water. The water is supplied to the faucet through a glass tube so shaped as to be entirely concealed within the stream of water flowing from the faucet.

After a short but brilliant career, during which he not only performed all over America and England, but also studied law and was admitted to the bar, Germain unfortunately became blind and was forced to retire. His assistant, Paul Fleming Gemmill, carried on his show and eventually became one of the few people to be listed in "Who's Who" twice, once under his own name as a distinguished professor of economics and author of scholarly books, and once as Paul Fleming, the magician.

There are other problems in conjuring today. In many ways the full evening show is the best format for a performance of conjuring. If the performer has the required amount of skill, imagination, and personality, the two and a half hours available to him allows him to use all the resources of the theater to create the proper air of mystery and to project the character he is playing to the audience.

However there are many reasons why most conjuring performances must be shorter than this, not the least of which are the economic reasons. Large illusions and scenery and assistants are very expensive today more so than ever before. But also the opportunity for such large shows just does not exist in today's theater. In addition to this there are magical plots and characterizations which are better presented in a short form, just as some stories are better when told as short stories rather than as long novels.

One famous conjurer created a short performance for vaudeville theaters by simply speeding up the pace of a long performance so that it could be done in a short time. Horace Goldin, a Polish born American conjurer, used to run through more tricks and illusions in one short performance than most conjurers would use in a lifetime. He was the first performer to publicize and make popular the now well-known trick of sawing a lady in half. As originally devised by Goldin, a hand saw was used to cut the lady into two sections. This slowed the pace of the show too much so Goldin developed a revised version in which he ran a power-driven circular saw blade through her.

Goldin's show had dash and surprise and excitement. It succeeded because the breakneck pace of the show fitted in with Goldin's personality. In one of his feats Goldin fired a pistol at a girl who was playing a piano on stage and not only the girl but the piano disappeared. If your attention had wandered you might have wondered what happened because the whole impossible event happened within seconds.

Goldin was in some ways an exception to the general rule that a long performance must have variety and a short performance must have unity. The shorter the performance the more closely it must adhere to its central theme. The conjurer's real task is to portray a character and the things he does must contribute to the portrayal without confusing the audience. The things he does must appear impossible but consistent.

Some performers have done this by expanding a short trick into a complete short act. Borrowing a hat from someone in the audience and removing some unlikely object from it was an old feat when Joseph Michael Hartz was born in Liverpool, England in 1836, but when Hartz became a conjurer he made a complete twenty-two minute act of removing articles from a borrowed hat. Hartz, originally a watchmaker, became a conjurer after seeing a performance by another ex-watchmaker, Robert-Houdin. Hartz was a perfectionist and developed many carefully planned routines, including one which derived its unity from the appearance of the equipment used. It was all made of glass. But his most famous routine was the one he called, "A Devil of a Hat."

Starting with a bare stage and several thin-topped tables Hartz would borrow a hat, actually planted in the audience, show the hat to be empty and then produce from it, without ever leaving the stage, a quantity of silks, twenty silver goblets, eighteen glass goblets, a wig, seven cigar boxes, a cage and canary, enough playing cards to fill six hats, a hundred yards of sash ribbon, seven glass lanterns each containing a lighted candle, a life size doll, a skull, ten champagne bottles, a porcelain bowl, and a glass bowl filled with water and goldfish. To the audience the whole thing seemed like a miracle because Hartz made no false motions. All his actions were confined to removing items from the hat and placing them on the tables. Hartz had a great many trick methods of introducing items into a hat under cover of a long series of natural moves.

Other performers have given unity and coherence to their acts by restricting their performance to one class of objects. Thomas Nelson Downs of Marshalltown Iowa became famous all over the world as the "King of Coins." Although Downs was a very versatile man and wrote a famous textbook on general conjuring, he concentrated in his publicity and his performances on magic with coins. The chief part of his act was known as "The Miser's Dream" and consisted of the production of an apparently unlimited number of coins from thin air. Despite repeated evidence that his hands were empty, he found coins everywhere. Borrowing a hat from one of the orchestra members, he would show that it was empty, then show that his hands were empty, and proceed to produce money from nowhere and put it in the hat. The act derived unity from the constantly repeated production of coins, and variety from the varied sleights he performed with them. Some of the coins he produced were thrown into the hat in the normal way, some were thrown in magically through the bottom of the hat. Some were passed mysteriously from one hand to the other. Some were magically passed from one hand to the other through his knees, and at one point in the routine forty coins were vanished and later reproduced from the bare hands.

Although Downs had many imitators, not all the performers of routines with coins have been imitators of T. Nelson Downs. The basic plot of the continuous production of coins was old even in his day. It is a natural because everyone is interested in the properties used, and the repetitive but varied productions can be used to build up to a finish much as Ravel did with music in his "Bolero."

New Yorker Al Flosso makes of the "Miser's Dream" one of the greatest comedy routines in conjuring. By getting a small boy up from the audience to assist him and then finding coins in the boy's hair, elbows, pockets, and every other impossible location while continuously talking to him and the audience in the voice of a carnival barker, Al reduces audiences to helpless laughter. Although Al Flosso uses a children's sand pail rather than a top hat to catch the coins, the basic plot of the routine and some of the sleight of hand is similar to Downs act. But the characterization and the effect on the audience is entirely different. Not only does Al Flosso not imitate anyone else, no one else has succeeded in imitating him.

Coins are not the only everyday objects that can be conjured with and made the properties for a specialty act. A conjurer named Gus Fowler was very successful in vaudeville with a seventeen minute act using nothing but clocks and watches. Nate Leipzig became an international celebrity performing with nothing but a deck of playing cards. Ade Duval developed an act using nothing but silk handkerchiefs finishing with a production of silks so tremendous that, when he played the Radio City Music Hall in New York, he was able to cover the stage and enlist the help of the

Al Flosso and a member of the audience.

Horace Goldin extends a hand
through a friend.

Rockettes to pick them up. He almost abandoned the act when he heard one of the spectators at the Palladium in London say, "That bloke with the rags wasn't half bad." All Duval could think of was the endless round of hours spent by himself and his assistants packing, folding, cleaning, and producing silks, and hearing them referred to as rags almost broke his heart.

Other conjurers have worked out acts in which they specialized in feats with billiard balls, ducks, rope, water, and cigarettes. Some people have begun to think that the only way to be original is to perform with some type of object that no one else has thought of using. One almost desperate man even took up performing levitation with a sledge hammer instead of a girl.

But the wisest performers realize that the greatest conjuring act possible is one in which the attention is on the performer, rather than on his properties. And even with today's problems for the conjurer, this can still be done.

Sleight of Hand
and Cardini

PROBABLY the highest form of conjuring entertainment is the pure sleight of hand performance using everyday objects and creating illusions by the skillful use of the body and mind. This was the original form of conjuring and has always been the most effective form for close-up performances, but it was not until the mid-nineteenth century that it seemed possible for large audiences. Today, it is almost the only kind being done.

A German conjurer, Wiljalba Frikell, discovered by accident that a sleight of hand performance could be enjoyed by a large audience. His equipment was destroyed in a fire, and could not be replaced quickly. True to the tradition that the show must go on, he performed without equipment, using only the skill of his hands. He not only astounded his audience, but he astounded himself; for he found that his show was better received than it had been before. He therefore abandoned the use of equipment and continued to perform pure sleight of hand.

109

Frikell soon had many imitators, most of them unsuccessful, for the pure sleight of hand performance is difficult to do well. It must be relatively short, for it is limited in scope by the size of the objects handled. Because it is short, it is difficult to establish the performer as an interesting personality in the minds of the audience.

One performer solved this problem in an unusual way. When José-Anténor Gago y Zavala, a Chilean nobleman who had lost 800,000 francs at Monte Carlo, became a conjurer in France he performed under the name of "l'Homme Masqué." By keeping his identity a secret, he gave himself an identity. He was a well-educated and graceful man who performed a clever sleight of hand act, but no small part of his success was due to the air of mystery created by the mask. Obviously concealing something increases interest in the thing concealed.

The period after the first World War brought forth the greatest sleight of hand performer of all time, a man who was to have more influence on conjuring than any man since Robert-Houdin. Richard Pitchford, born in Wales, developed a stage personality so brilliant that it revolutionized twentieth century conjuring. Under the name of Cardini he became internationally famous by creating the most nearly perfect conjuring act ever to be seen. Silently, using nothing but a deck of playing cards, several billiard balls, a pack of cigarettes, a cigar, and a pipe, he held audiences spellbound in the largest theaters of the world.

When he was a small boy in Wales, Cardini saw a performance by Chung Ling Soo, and a spark of interest in conjuring began to burn. His mother ran a boarding house for actors, and he learned some card sleights from an actor who also did some conjuring. He learned more about card manipulation from a book written by T. Nelson Downs, and continued to practice at it when he was in the British army in France during the first World War. Because it was cold in the trenches, he practiced doing card manipulations wearing gloves. He was encouraged in this unconventional military activity by his commanding officer. When he became famous many years later, Cardini was still manipulating cards wearing gloves, and by then looked very much like his old commanding officer, an English gentleman with close cropped mustache and monocle.

While recovering from a severe case of shell shock in a hospital in Southampton, England, Cardini asked for playing cards and a pair of gloves. The hospital psychiatrist asked him why he wanted the gloves, and he said he needed them to produce cards from the air. This resulted in Cardini's being transferred to a mental hospital, where he was allowed to have the cards and gloves. He continued to practice at sleight of hand and insisted that he wanted to be a magician, which for some time resulted in his being kept in the mental hospital. Finally one of the psychiatrists saw him perform and realized that he was not suffering from delusions but was a very clever performer. Released then from the hospital, he set out on the slow process of building up a perfect conjuring act.

When he first began to perform, Cardini tried all sorts of conjuring routines. He performed with silk handkerchiefs, thimbles, flag staves, and even tried ventriloquism. Because he had a superb sense of what fit into his act, and because he was determined to be the greatest in his field, he continually asked for suggestions and was able to accept the good and reject the bad. A theater manager suggested that he wear top hat, tails, and an opera cape. He did. Then it was suggested that it did not look right to wear the top hat all during his performance, so he had an assistant come on to take the hat. He amused people at a party by pantomiming the part of a drunk, so he put the pantomime in the act.

In its ultimate form, Cardini's act began with a page, played by his wife, walking up the aisle of the theater calling out, "paging Mr. Cardini—paging Mr. Cardini—". Cardini would then saunter on stage impeccably dressed in full evening clothes with Inverness cape and top hat, reading a newspaper, with the orchestra playing "Three o'clock in the Morning." He appeared to be a somewhat foppish English gentleman on his way home from a late party, after having had more than several whiskies and soda. He looked up from his paper and noticed the page, to whom he then handed the newspaper. Suddenly a fan of playing cards appeared in his hand. He adjusted his monocle to look at it, as amazed as anyone in the audience. He dropped the cards into the newspaper in the page's hand, but another fan of cards appeared. He seemed to be seeing things in his mildly confused alcoholic condition, but curiously enough the things he saw were also visible to the audience.

Cards continued to plague him by appearing in bunches even though he was wearing gloves. He handed his top hat to the page and more cards appeared. He adjusted his monocle and more cards

Cardini as the drunk to whom everything happens.

appeared. After he removed his gloves still more cards appeared. His pantomime was so perfect that it appeared that these things happened to him, not that he was a clever manipulator who caused them to happen. This was one of Cardini's greatest innovations. He cast himself as the victim of the magic, rather than its master.

After producing more cards, or rather after more cards appeared mysteriously in his hands, he suddenly realized that he was holding a billiard ball instead of another fan of cards. He peered at it through his monocle, tossed it in the air and it changed color. It multiplied to two and then multiplied again.

He was so unnerved by all this that he took a cigarette from a case and lit it. After several puffs he threw it away, but to his amazement he discovered that he still had a cigarette in his mouth. The cigarettes began to bedevil him the way the cards and billiard balls had. No matter how he tried to dispose of them, he still had lit cigarettes in his hand, until he was finally even more astonished to discover that the cigarette had changed to a cigar. As he walked off stage, the cigar changed to a large calabash pipe.

Cardini's act was enormously successful. He performed many times at all the greatest theaters of the world, the Palace in New York when it was the goal of all performers, the Radio City Music Hall, which built its entire show around him, the Palladium in London, and many others.

But to the time of his retirement he refused to perform on television, and he had excellent reasons. In addition to genius, a conjuring act like Cardini's requires many years of hard work and experimentation. Although it is not seen to its best advantage on television, it is seen by an almost unbelievably large number of people. More people may see one television show than could be crowded into the Radio City Music Hall in fifty years. It is bad business to spend twenty years developing a perfect twelve minute act and then show it to your entire potential audience on one night.

Mental Magic

MOST CONJURING assumes the existence of the normal five senses and shows that the mind can be deceived by the information furnished through those senses. There is also a branch of conjuring, usually called mental magic, that endeavors to show that the mind can reach correct conclusions and communicate with other minds without using the five senses. Mental magic uses the same methods as all other conjuring but strives for a different effect.

The second sight act of Pinetti's was an early example of this type of conjuring. Similar performances, using various methods of communication between the two performers, have been given ever since. Robert-Houdin is thought to have invented a silent code, using gestures to convey information to an assistant on stage. Robert Heller used a telegraph apparatus concealed in a couch to describe to his blindfolded, on stage assistant, sitting on the couch, the articles being shown by spectators. More recent performers have used electronic equipment. Karl Germain used a thread and

115

the Morse code to communicate with a blindfolded assistant by touch.

Although the general fact that such codes exist is known to many people, a pair of skilled performers can communicate so quickly and easily that they really seem to possess some sixth sense. Many intelligent people have been convinced that telepathy is possible after watching such a team. You might think that by observation you could see through the code being used, but all good conjurers vary their methods so that any theory you may arrive at is destroyed by the next thing that is done.

There is one problem in mental magic: a really good performance may induce a belief in something that is false. No one believes that a sleight of hand performer produces billiard balls from nothing. But in the field of mental magic the age old battle between conjurer and charlatan is still being fought.

Mental magic has been especially popular in recent years because of the research being done by many scientists in the field of extra-sensory perception. People may be capable of seeing through some sense other than the eyes, of communicating with another person by telepathy, of seeing the future, or of moving physical objects with their minds. But the evidence for these abilities is not clear; and if they exist at all, they exist rarely and feebly. Too firm a belief in them provides a golden opportunity for charlatans.

Perhaps you do not believe there are trick ways of predicting the future. There are many. One is the ancient one of making prediction so ambiguous that it may be interpreted as true no matter what happens. Another is to make many predictions of things that are likely to happen and call attention to the ones that work out, forgetting the others. A future event may even be arranged by a predictor, as in the case of a mindreader who predicted petty crimes by having his assistant commit the crimes. A prediction may be made after an event by switching one envelope for another, the second containing the prediction allegedly made in the first. One gambler had an unusual variant on this. He carried a portable radio in his hat and made bets after a race was over, when he knew the results but his victim did not.

Seeing without the use of the eyes has been demonstrated by many conjurers, perhaps most brilliantly by a Pakistani conjurer, Kuda Bux. Even the most skeptical spectator must agree that it is impossible for Kuda Bux to see when large lumps of paste are put in his eye sockets, which are further covered with pads of cotton, and heavy strips of cloth wound about his head in all directions. They also must agree that he does see somehow, when he next shows that he can copy anything they write on a blackboard, even correcting them when they forget to dot an *i* or cross a *t*. He shoots at and hits targets with a rifle, and once even rode in the six-day bicycle race in Madison Square Garden. When the cloths are removed from his head, the paste must be dug out of his eye sockets piece by piece.

Dr. Harlan Tarbell, artist, conjurer, lecturer, and writer of the most monumental work on conjuring in the English language, used to perform a somewhat similar feat, but he gave it his own individual touch. He pretended to be able to see through his fingertips and was able to describe minutely anything near them while his eyes were blindfolded.

Perhaps the nearest approach to real mind reading in a public exhibition was given by Washington Irving Bishop, a so-called contact mind reader. Bishop would allow his audience to hide something and then, holding the wrist of anyone who knew where it was hidden, he would promptly find the object. Bishop lived before the time of the lie detector but his method was somewhat similar. He had very sensitive perceptions and could tell by the subject's reaction whether he was headed away from or toward the hidden object.

Many conjurers have been expert both in conjuring with physical objects and in performing mental magic. Al Baker, a witty and inventive conjurer contributed many brilliant ideas to the field of mental magic, although his performances were devoted more to effects with cards, paper, silks, and even chewing gum than they were to mind reading. Some of Mr. Baker's telepathic tricks were performed over the telephone without his so much as touching the phone or speaking over it.

Theodore Anneman, the proprietor for some years of a magazine for conjurers called *The Jinx* was another conjurer who was greatly interested in mental trickery. Although Anneman was an expert with cards and performed the bullet catching trick with great success, mental magic best fitted his belief that conjuring should be so convincing that it could be accepted as real by an audience.

Anneman was probably correct in thinking that in a scientific age the most mysterious conjuring would be that which dealt with unknown powers of the mind, but he himself did not have the nerves of steel necessary to make this type of performance successful on a grand scale. It took Joseph Dunninger, a master showman with the same drive and dominating personality that made Houdini great, to show for over fifty years, that such a performance could grip the attention of the whole nation.

At the peak of his career Dunninger had one of the nation's most popular television shows, on which he read the minds of the studio audience and performed such impossible feats as reading the serial number of a dollar bill selected at random and kept in the possession of the chief of the United States Secret Service.

Dunninger first became interested in magic when he was a child and saw Harry Kellar perform. Before he was twenty years old he was performing under the name of "Mysterious Dunninger, the Illusionist with the Somewhat Different Act." Like Houdini, Dunninger wanted to become a suave and polished actor with a large illusion show complete with elaborate equipment and beautiful girl assistants. But like Houdini, Dunninger found that he was more successful in the sort of performance in which one individual challenges the audience to a battle of wits. Houdini challenged anyone to handcuff, bind, or confine him so he could not escape, and Dunninger challenged anyone to show that he did not read minds. Both men challenged spirit mediums on many occasions to do anything that they could not either duplicate or explain by normal means. Both men have been thought to have some supernormal power by eminent men, in spite of disclaiming any such power.

The performances of both Houdini and Dunninger illustrate in an extreme way something that is true with respect to all successful performances of conjuring. It is necessary for the conjurer to dominate his audience. The effect of magic cannot be created in the minds of an audience without the intelligent and undivided attention of the audience. There is no equivalent to dinner music in the field of conjuring. This domination need not be as obvious as in the cases of Houdini and Dunninger, it may be much more subtle, but it must exist. Cardini, for example, dominates an audience, not by being forceful, but by using his uncanny sense of timing. His performance is such a series of surprises that the audience is thrown off guard and is forced to pay strict attention without realizing that they are being controlled by the performer.

Did Dunninger really read the minds of his audience? In all conjuring, but particularly in mental magic, it is good psychology to keep the audience from finding out how it is done. This leaves open the possibility that the illusions witnessed are real, and increases interest. Intelligent people, however, realize that the conjurer is playing a game with them. Anyone who could really read minds could own the world. Anyone with the skill and knowledge of a Dunninger or a Houdini could own half the world if he were dishonest. Fortunately they were both honest men and used their talent to entertain.

Dunninger has done his part in combatting charlatanry by investigating spirit mediums and writing extensively on the dishonest methods used by many of them. Scientists investigating alleged supernormal feats of mediums have defined *telekinesis* as the ability of a medium to cause objects to move at a distance and *parakinesis* as the ability of a medium to cause unexplained motion of an object with which he or she is in contact. Dunninger is a practical man and once corrected the definitions to say that *telekinesis* is an object being moved by attaching a thread to it and *parakinesis* is shoving an object with a foot.

Some researchers in laboratories claim to have shown that the ability to control material objects by the mind exists. They say that statistical analysis shows that dice can be controlled by some people who can concentrate and cause certain numbers to turn up more often than they should. Another conjurer, John Scarne, pointed out that it is very strange that this ability does not show up in gambling casinos, where the customers are concentrating like mad while the casino employees are looking on in a state of bored detachment. Despite this unequal war of concentration, the casinos always win exactly in accord with statistical theory.

John Scarne

JOHN SCARNE, one of the cleverest men in the world with playing cards, has achieved international fame as an expert on gambling. Although not the first conjurer to expose the trickery of dishonest gamblers, Scarne is undoubtedly the greatest. He is the author of many books on the methods of dishonest gamblers and the rules to be followed by the individual who insists on gambling despite Scarne's most basic advice, which is "Don't Gamble." Scarne has devoted a large part of his life to an attempt to convince people that if they gamble they will either lose their money rapidly by being cheated, or slowly by the inexorable operation of mathematical laws, which give a favorable percentage to the operator of the gambling game or device.

Scarne grew up in an area where illegal gambling was almost as common as breathing. He learned card sleight of hand from card sharpers, worked for a man who manufactured marked cards and crooked dice, and hung out at carnivals where he learned all about the shell game and various other gambling swindles. Although he had a keen analytical mind and did well in mathematics, he left school after he finished the eighth grade and did not go to high school. He was interested only in gambling and in boxing with his friend Jim Braddock, who later became the heavyweight champion of the world.

At this point most sociologists would have predicted that Scarne would become a criminal. However as time went by it turned out that he was too honest to gamble. He began to realize that what he was really interested in was the exercise of skill to impress other people. For ten or twelve hours a day he practiced sleight of hand and began to invent card tricks that utilized the methods of the card cheats, not to fleece anyone, but to create spectacular conjuring tricks. Conjurers have long known that some of the most perfect sleight of hand with cards is performed by dishonest professional gamblers. This is true because the card cheat's very life may depend on his not being detected in manipulating a deck of cards.

Many conjurers have taken a professional interest in gambling sleight of hand and trick devices because of their ingenuity and indetectability, although most of them are not of much use to the conjurer who entertains large audiences. The fundamental purpose of gambling trickery is different from the fundamental purpose of conjuring trickery. The conjurer wants the effects he creates to be as spectacular as possible, at the risk of being detected by some small proportion of the audience. The gambler wants to be inconspicuous, with the least possible risk of being detected.

Scarne developed many card tricks that were a blend

of the phenomenal skill developed by the gamblers and the dazzling effect desired by the conjurer. He would have a card selected, marked, and replaced in the deck. Then Scarne would immediately hand the deck to the spectator, who would find that the card was no longer in the deck but was safely in Scarne's wallet in his inside coat pocket. He would shuffle and flourish a borrowed deck and then cut the four aces from the deck one by one. A marked card would disappear from the deck and turn up in Scarne's mouth.

Scarne's conjuring is entirely a demonstration of technical skill in sleight of hand. He scorns mechanical devices, stage properties, and acting technique. He has concentrated on dexterity, both of the hand and of the mind. How well he has succeeded may be judged by the fact that not only conjurers, but gamblers regard him with awe.

Because the card magic at which Scarne excels can only be properly appreciated close up, his performances in theaters and night clubs have been limited, but he has done thousands of performances at clubs and dinners and at private parties. He has entertained individuals as diverse as President Franklin D. Roosevelt and Arnold Rothstein, the notorious gambler. Roosevelt's favorite trick was the one in which Scarne produced a selected card from his mouth, and predictably enough, Rothstein's was the one in which Scarne cut to the aces in a shuffled and borrowed deck.

During the second world war, Scarne traveled all over the country to military camps and posts, giving lectures and demonstrations on ways of avoiding being cheated by dice and card sharpers. He found

John Scarne shows U. S. Senators a marked deck of cards.

that there was such a need for education in this field that he continued to give lectures and demonstrations after the war and wrote a number of books on gambling and conjuring and games.

Many other conjurers have written exposes of gambling methods; among them Robert-Houdin, J.N. Maskelyne, and Harry Houdini. But to these men gambling methods were a side interest. To Scarne they became a passion. He became the consultant on gambling to the Hilton and Sheraton hotels and to Laurance Rockefeller. He testified before a Senate Committee investigating Gambling and Organized Crime at which he showed Senator McClellan how to switch dice. He made numerous television appearances on interview shows. He became recognized as one of the world's foremost authorities on games and gambling, while not only advising people not to gamble, but showing them by demonstration how they can be cheated, and proving mathematically that they cannot win even if the game is honest.

Mulholland and Tarbell

CONJURING today is epitomized by John Mulholland, a proponent of a dignified and intellectual approach. His performance is not a visual symphony like Cardini's, nor a challenge to the audience in the manner of Houdini or Dunninger. Rather his performances are lectures on the history and art of conjuring, illustrated with articles that can be carried with him conveniently.

Mulholland's public performances have included such items as the cut and restored rope, the cut and restored handkerchief, the passage of cards from one envelope to another, the vanishing of a selected card and its discovery in a cigarette, thimble manipulations, the vanishing bird cage, tricks with silks, and the Chinese linking rings. He believes in performing relatively small feats and expanding them to large illusions by the use of the spoken word. Because of this theory Mulholland has been subjected to some good-natured ribbing by other conjurers. During ceremonies in connection with the presentation of an award to Mulholland, one performer announced that he would

127

produce a thousand flowers from a paper cone. He then produced one flower and offered it as a sample of what the full production would look like if he chose to do it.

Despite such kidding, it is quite clear that Mulholland's theory is true. To create the maximum impression on his audience a conjurer must seem to be using only a small part of the power he possesses. If his talent is seemingly stretched to its limit by the vanishing of a small coin, he creates less of an impression on a spectator than if he picks up the coin and vanishes it merely to illustrate how he could if he wished vanish a rabbit or a horse or an automobile or anything else. The theory works handsomely for close-up performances or performances in places with poor staging facilities. In a large and elaborate theater a logical spectator might wonder why the performer did not vanish the horse. Although he is noted for his skill in sleight of hand, John Mulholland's greatest fame has been achieved through the use of words. He was for almost twenty-five years the editor of the greatest magazine ever to be published for conjurers, the *Sphinx*. Some magazines are meant to be read and thrown away. The *Sphinx* was different. It not only published the best information on technical methods, but also the greatest collection of biographical, historical and cultural information on conjuring ever gathered. The *Sphinx* published woodcuts and paintings relating to conjuring, articles on conjurers' bookplates, articles on the psychology of conjuring, reminiscenses and predictions by well-known conjurers, and articles for book collectors and historians. When the editors of the *Encyclopaedia Britannica* wanted some-

John Mulholland in three guises

one to write their section on conjuring and magic, they unhesitatingly chose Mulholland.

Mulholland's interest in conjuring began at the age of five. He became an instructor at Columbia University's Horace Mann School for Boys before he became a full time professional conjurer. It was at the suggestion of Dr. Brander Matthews, a famous professor at Columbia and an authority on the drama, that Mulholland adopted the lecture approach.

Late in his career Harry Houdini decided to include in his shows a lecture on false spirit phenomena. Although he was internationally famous, he realized that his formal education was poor and he was afraid that his poor grammar would dull the effect of his lectures. So he did something a lesser man would never have done. He contacted Columbia University and asked them to recommend someone who could teach him how to lecture. The University recommended Mulholland and the two men spent much time together exchanging information. They each learned a great deal and became firm friends.

Mulholland's influence not only helped shape Houdini's lectures, but helped shape the entire present-day world of conjuring. Mulholland's great contributions to conjuring were in increasing its acceptance by the most highly educated segment of the population, in creating interest in conjuring through his books for young people, and in providing a professional magazine that raised the cultural level of conjuring.

Of course Mulholland is not the only author to have shaped the course of modern conjuring. Jean Hugard, an Australian conjurer, and Lewis Ganson, a British army officer, have been two of the most prolific authors of technical books for the modern conjurer. But the most prolific author of all was Harlan Tarbell.

Tarbell, at one time the art editor of *Photoplay* magazine, was a very skilled lecturer on conjuring. During the nineteen twenties he wrote a correspondence course for amateur conjurers. Originally the course was planned as a series of lessons on pocket tricks for business men; but when it was discovered that there was considerable interest in a full course in conjuring, it was expanded and made into a very complete set of lessons with the object of making the student into a full professional.

Dr. Tarbell's course was so successful that it became a textbook for magicians all over the world. One American conjurer traveling in India offered to purchase some tricks from a Hindu fakir and was amazed to discover that the Hindu had learned the tricks from the Tarbell course. Copies of the course were even purchased by witch doctors in Africa, who requested that it be sent in a plain wrapper so their believers would not find out that their magic came from Chicago.

There was only one bad thing about Dr. Tarbell's course. His lessons were so thorough and so well done that performers all over the world appeared doing the same tricks in the same way and even saying the same words. This was not really what Tarbell sought to accomplish.

What conjuring really needs is originality, talent, and a stage. Dr. Tarbell's work, which is a six volume set of books, is invaluable as an encyclopedia, recording the original creations of many people. And it is best used when a talented person takes it as a basis for his own original performances.

Television

THERE ARE probably more conjurers now than there ever have been before, but there are no great conjurers with elaborate shows in the tradition of Kellar, Thurston, and Blackstone. There are even very few perfect short acts like Cardini's. The reason is that it is no longer possible to perfect a performance by working in small time theaters. The only theater in the United States that presents variety entertainment is the Radio City Music Hall, in New York City, which is scarcely the place to start in show business.

Under the circumstances, it is not surprising that the number of professional conjurers has declined. To see good sleight of hand performers it is almost necessary to travel to London or Paris. To be sure, conjurers are seen occasionally on television variety shows, but television cannot furnish the conditions that allow a good conjurer to create magic. To be truly impressive, a miracle like the appearance of something or its disappearance, must be seen first hand. To be thrilling, an escape must be seen when it occurs. Seeing it on

132

magnetic tape will not do. The conjurer's art really exists only in the place and at the time that he creates it.

In addition to this, the fast and frantic pace of television makes it difficult for the performer to create the atmosphere he needs. After a performance at a conjurer's society meeting Chang, a venerable, clever, and charming Chinese conjurer was asked to do a two minute performance on a television variety show. One of his friends shook his head sadly and said, "He takes longer than that to bow."

On television the audience's attention is not under the control of the performer alone. The cameraman and the director also direct the attention of the audience, and unless they too are conjurers there is apt to be confusion. A television director attempts to avoid monotony by shifting from one camera to another and by shifting between long shots and close-ups. This can result in an extreme close-up at the time of a crucial move that the performer is trying to cover up, or at the opposite extreme, the performer's hands may be completely out of the picture, leading the spectators to think that something is going on that they are not seeing and that this explains the trick. Large illusions are difficult to do on television because it is hard to convince the audience that they are not done by trick photography.

Although performances of conjuring for adults are not frequent on television, many performers have done series shows for children and been very successful. Children are more interested in the story that is told to accompany a trick than they are in a perfectly routined and performed sleight of hand performance.

This makes it possible to vary the show more easily. Among the successful performers of this type of show have been Richard DuBois, Don Alan, Don Lawton, and Gerri Larsen.

Probably the foremost performer of conjuring on television is a Baltimorean, Milbourne Christopher. Mr. Christopher has appeared many times on most of the variety and interview shows on television. He is one of the most versatile conjurers who has ever lived and has been able to conquer television by continually changing his material. He has done literally thousands of different tricks on hundreds of different programs.

Early in his career Christopher specialized in tricks done with rope and invented a way of stretching a small piece of rope to a length of many yards. But narrow specialization was too confining for a man of Milbourne Christopher's personality and intellectual curiosity. He has since performed sleight of hand, illusions, mental magic, close-up magic, and every other type of conjuring. He has performed in almost forty different countries, in five different languages and has written fifteen books on magic, some technical and some historical. He is one of the world's greatest collectors of books, posters, pictures, and memorabilia of conjuring.

Christopher has performed before more people than Robert-Houdin, Herrmann, Kellar, Thurston, and Houdini, put together. If he is less well known in his age than they were in theirs it is the fault of our age, and not his. If Shakespeare had been a television writer he never would have written *Hamlet*, but he would still have been Shakespeare.

Magic Today

YOU MAY wonder how there can be more conjurers today than ever before when there are fewer public performances. Conjuring is not only fascinating to watch, but fascinating to perform. Fooling people with apparent miracles has all the thrill of being an international jewel thief or a secret agent without any of the risks. Everyone would like to have the power to work miracles, and conjuring gives anyone willing to work at it the ability to feel for the moment like a miracle worker.

No one knows how many people have attempted to perform conjuring tricks, but a very high percentage of boys try it at some point. Usually their interest is sparked by seeing a good conjurer and fueled by reading a book on conjuring or being shown how to do some simple trick by a friend or relative. Most people who try this find that fooling people to entertain them is not as easy as they first thought. A small percentage continue and become amateur conjurers. There are perhaps fifty thousand such amateurs.

To about ten per cent of this fifty thousand conjuring is such an all-absorbing passion that they spend all the time they can spare from their everyday occupation at some phase of conjuring. These are the people who invent new conjuring deceptions, organize and join societies of magicians, publish books and magazines for conjurers, organize conventions and benefit shows for conjurers, perform as semi-professionals, and generally use their diverse talents for the benefit of conjuring. In this group are surgeons, lawyers, business executives, actors, writers, police officers, publishers, florists, and people from every profession and occupation imaginable.

Among amateur conjurers have been such famous writers as Charles Dickens; Lewis Carroll; Fulton Oursler, the former editor of the *Reader's Digest*; Walter Gibson, the author of "The Shadow"; Bruce Elliott, author and editor; and many others. Among actor conjurers have been Harold Lloyd, Chester Morris, Orson Welles, Milton Berle, and Carroll Baker.

The elite among conjurers are of course the full time professionals. They may be outranked in the outside world by the distinguished amateurs, but the people who are truly interested in conjuring live in a world of their own, an international fraternity with its own celebrities. A real conjuring enthusiast would rather be Cardini than president.

Conjurers have invented a whole world of outlets for conjuring performances to replace the disappearing variety theater. There are numerous societies of conjurers, the largest in the United States being the Society of American Magicians and the International Brother-

Dai Vernon performing for Loring Campbell
and John Mulholland at the Magic Castle.

The Magic Castle from the outside.

hood of Magicians. Each of these runs an annual convention with performances for conjurers during the day and public shows at night. In addition there are local branches of each society that run both private and public performances. There are also many smaller societies, The Magician's Guild, the Magician's Alliance of Eastern States, the Pacific Coast Association of Magicians, etc., which run conventions, Annual shows, Ladies Nights and other performances.

Many local associations sponsor lectures for people interested in learning conjuring. There is a private club in Los Angeles called The Magic Castle, founded by Milt and Bill Larsen for the benefit of conjurers and those who love conjuring, which provides food, drink, and close-up magic in an old Charles Addams style house. The conjuring is done by several house conjurers and by the members and guests.

When you add to all these the similar organizations and opportunities that exist in Britain and on the continent, it becomes apparent that a performer can almost make a permanent career of performing for other performers. And there are such performers. Possibly the most famous of these is Dai Vernon, who is almost unknown to the public at large but is revered by other conjurers and referred to affectionately as "The Professor." Vernon is a great authority and is such a perfectionist that he works out conjuring effects with the same devotion that Toscanini brought to music.

This retreat into a world of its own has served conjuring well during the eclipse of live show business brought about by the motion pictures and television. It bears a certain similarity to the preservation of literature and art in the monasteries and castles of the Middle Ages. For conjuring is an ancient and indestructible art, and someday people will realize again that conjuring can be used to say things to people that they cannot understand in words. It is one of the few arts that is not even limited by the possible.

The great conjurer of the future, like the ones of the past, will be someone who is not only well-versed in the technical methods used to create illusion, but is also skilled in the craft of the actor. This may sound obvious, but unless one has tried it one does not realize how one can become swamped in technical methods developed by other people and forget that conjuring is really a branch of the theater.

The only way to keep from being overwhelmed by technical details is to sift out fundamental principles, see how they have been used by others, and then apply them to create the conjuring of the future.

Invent Your Own Magic

CREATIVITY in conjuring is of two general types. There is the creativity of the inventor of methods and apparatus, and there is the creativity of the author-director who first visualizes a character to be played, then devises situations and plots for the character to play, and finally rehearses and refines the performance, and inserts bits of "business" to enliven it. The conjurer's chief difficulty and at the same time his chief glory is that he must be both creator and performer.

There are two ways to avoid creativity. Copying someone's act outright, thereby flattering him and insuring the copier's failure. Signor Blitz, a nineteenth century conjurer, once complained that there were thirteen other men not only doing his act, but using variations of his name, such as Signor Blitz Jr., Signor Blitz's Nephew, Signor Blitz, The Mysterious, and even Signor Blitz, The Original. Needless to say, none of the imitators were successful, though Signor Blitz retired with a comfortable fortune. Cardini has been probably the most imitated conjurer of the twentieth century. At one time he jokingly suggested that he intended holding a convention in Madison Square Garden for all the people doing his act.

The other way, the only ethical way to avoid creativity, is to purchase routines for individual tricks from magic dealers or take them from books. These routines may be obtained complete with method, apparatus, plot, patter, and even suggestions for costuming and music.

This method has some of the disadvantages of the first. Since what the performer is doing is in each part identical to what many other conjurers are doing, audiences are likely to conclude that all are copiers like Signor Blitz, the Original. It even has a disadvantage that is not present in outright copying. If a series of tricks are presented, each element of the program has no relation to the other elements of the program, and each part of the program requires the projection of a different character. The performer may find himself trying to do one trick as a Mexican peon, the next as a night club comedian, and the next as a pseudo-scientific lecturer. Anyone with the acting ability to carry off this sort of performance, should probably desert conjuring for straight acting. It pays better.

How do you arrive at the stage where you can design your own act and present it? The first thing to do is to develop the acting ability, the sense of misdirection and the dexterity required for successful conjuring. But you probably will want to do something for your friends long before you have mastered these arts. So you can buy a trick or two and mix them with a display of skill. Even some of the simplest sleight of hand moves, however, require considerable practice because

they can be done perfectly. Therefore it is probably
wise to start by practicing decorative manipulations
that are not concealed sleight of hand moves. This
includes such manipulations as the coin roll, card fans,
and one-handed cuts. This will give you practice in
handling the sort of objects used in close-up magic,
increase your confidence, and give you some manifestations of skill that you can mix in with simple
self-working tricks to make up early performances.
If you are known to be a beginner and show tricks
without demonstrating some sort of skill, your audience is likely to conclude, rightly enough, that the
effects you are showing work themselves; this gives
them a lesser opinion of your performance and helps
them puzzle out the secret methods you are using.
Later when you are really expert you may want to
eliminate from your routine any open show of skill
in order to make your magic more mysterious.

If you find that you enjoy performing, you should
begin to practice some of the sleights that have shown
their worth over hundreds of years of performances,
such as the palming of cards from the top of the deck,
the palming of small objects in being passed from
hand to hand, and the move with cards known as
"the pass." This will greatly increase your repertoire
of feats and enable you to make some of the self
working tricks more deceptive. You will for example
be able to reduce your dependence on things like
trick decks of cards that do self-working feats and start
to perform mystifying feats with ordinary cards. At the
same time you should experiment and practice at
developing the technique of misdirecting and directing
attention.

You should also learn to perform some of the classic feats of conjuring and study them to understand why they have lasted so long. The best trick for this is the cups and balls. Any trick that can entertain people for over two thousand years is well worth studying. Some authorities on conjuring have claimed that it is impossible to learn conjuring without doing the cups and balls. Others have said that the cups and balls trick is the original one from which all other conjuring developed. Although these statements may be overenthusiastic, it is true that a great deal can be learned about vanishes, productions, transfers, multiplication, and penetration as conjuring effects by learning to perform a routine with the cups and balls.

Another thing you will learn by practicing the cups and balls is the necessity of rehearsing until you can perform without consciously thinking about what you are doing. Any uncertainty or confusion on the part of the performer is fatal to illusion. This does not mean that you should rush through things. One of the most important things you must learn is timing, and this can only be learned by performing for an audience. Admittedly this presents a difficulty. You should not perform before an audience until your performance is perfect, but you can only perfect it by performing for audiences. The only solution is to practice before audiences of your friends and relatives. This is rather hard on them, but it cannot be helped. The trick must be practiced until you are absolutely sure of everything in it, including manipulation, pantomime, and speech.

A poor trick will be a poor trick no matter how well rehearsed, but a good one cannot be good unless it is well rehearsed. Kellar was such a perfectionist that he flew into a rage at his assistants if so much as one table was placed out of position by one step on his stage. Thurston used to hold a meeting of his entire company after each performance and go over any mistakes that had been made so they would never happen again. David Devant was once asked by an amateur conjurer how many tricks he knew. The amateur added that he himself knew hundreds. Devant thought the question over and replied that he only knew eight tricks. This was his way of pointing out that a smattering of knowledge is much less useful than thorough knowledge of a limited number of things.

As you progress in magic you will undoubtedly try many of the tricks described in books and many sold by dealers. This experience will be very valuable to you if you keep in mind that you must do the tricks exactly as they are described in order to learn as much as you can. Doing so is similar to following a chess game played by two masters in order to learn something to improve your own game. But you must not think that you can form a good conjuring act by learning tricks through set recipes and stringing them together. A good act comes only through study of the fundamentals of misdirection and the principles of deception, and then using these to find out what direction your own creative efforts should take.

There are two approaches to developing a magic act, once the basic skills have been learned. The first is the inventive. This means that the ingenious device or method to fool people, comes first and then the conjurer devises a presentation for the invention. This is the most common method used to create new conjuring. It is especially favored by amateurs who bring specialized knowledge to their hobby. One man may be a professional chemist and therefore well qualified to use chemical principles to create startling effects. Another may be a watchmaker and invent ingenious mechanisms to vanish or levitate or change articles. Another may be interested in dexterity because he is a surgeon and invent new and ingenious sleight of hand moves.

One of the easiest paths to invention is to apply an old method to a new object. A method once used to vanish fishbowls is now used to vanish a radio. Another way is to apply new scientific devices and principles from the world at large to conjuring uses. Mind reading acts have been and are performed sometimes with the aid of miniature transmitters and receivers. In recent years, now that very powerful miniature permanent magnets have become technically possible, magic inventors have been using them in all kinds of tricks. They have been concealed in coins, dice, playing cards, and almost any other obviously non-magnetic object you can think of. This makes it possible to conceal objects by allowing them to adhere to any convenient magnetic metal surface. The principle has even been used to simulate a magical penetration. An object is placed on a non-magnetic surface openly, while at the same time a duplicate is secretly placed on the other, unseen side of the surface. The two objects adhere to each other through the surface and allow the hands to be shown empty. When the visible object is removed by palming or by covering it with something containing a stronger magnet, the hidden one falls, apparently having penetrated the surface.

Anyone with a moderate amount of technical ingenuity can think up many variations on this and on any other method or principle or piece of apparatus used in conjuring. There are all sorts of possibilities. You can try converting a vanish into a production by doing it in reverse. You can look up ancient tricks and see how they can be converted to modern objects. You can combine known principles to produce an apparently new effect. Sometimes an old principle can be merely carried farther to create something new. The possibilities of invention in conjuring are as limitless as the possibilities of invention in general.

The other creative approach to conjuring is the dramatic one. This means the visualization of a magical plot or effect first and then the finding, buying, or inventing of the technical means to act out the plot or effect for an audience. This is by far the best way to create new conjuring because it recognizes that the purpose of conjuring is the entertainment of audiences. By visualizing the effect first, before working out the method of stimulating it, the chance of creating a performance that is interesting to audiences because it involves an interesting character playing the lead role in a series of consistent and interesting playlets is increased.

Here too, as in technical inventiveness, there is no limit to how far creativity can go. Not all things are possible, but it is possible to create the appearance of almost anything, no matter how impossible, or improbable, the thing may be. What could be more impossible than causing a lady to float in air at the wave

of a hand? Maskelyne, Kellar, Thurston, and Blackstone did it. What could be more improbable than
that Houdini should escape after being welded in a
steel tank?

There are many more impossible things that can be
acted out, and someone will do it. No one knows now
what they are nor does anyone know who will do them,
but the art of conjuring has been progressing for thousands of years and it will continue to progress as long
as there are people with the intelligence to be interested
in things they do not understand. The important thing
is that interested people begin at the beginning and
learn first the basic skills needed, then progress to
lively, intelligent performances.

Misdirection

ANY PERFORMER must be able to secure the attention of an audience and hold that attention while he is performing. Because he must perform many actions secretly, the conjurer must not only hold the attention of his audience but at the same time direct their attention away from the actions he wants to conceal.

Attention itself is one of the strongest forms of misdirection. Harry Kellar once said that if he could get the complete attention of an audience he could have his assistant bring an elephant on stage unseen. It is very difficult for the mind to pay attention to more than one thing at a time. In doing close-up conjuring you can often direct the attention of the spectator away from your hands simply by asking a question. In answering the spectator instinctively looks at you and is no longer able to pay strict attention to your hands.

The eyes may be used to direct attention. A spectator will tend to look at whatever you look at. If you are accomplishing some secret move, you must never look at it. Look at the audience, look at the hand not performing the secret motion, but never look where you don't want the audience to look.

Since a moving object attracts more attention than a stationary one, if you want to direct attention to something move it. If you have a card palmed in the right hand, then move the left hand to divert attention, but the move must be for some plausible reason such as placing the rest of the deck of cards on a table. If you must move the hand containing the palmed card, then let the move be covered by some plausible action. If you must place the card in your pocket, reach in the pocket to remove some other object that is necessary at that point. However don't reach in the pocket to remove some imaginary magic powder. This has been done by many amateur conjurers, almost invariably with poor results. It is not logical enough to be convincing.

In general all secret actions in a conjuring trick must be covered by actions that are necessary to the playlet you are performing for the audience. This playlet should be interesting in itself, and should logically have as its climax the magical illusion you are presenting. If the playlet includes a false explanation of the magical phenomenon you are presenting, as it sometimes does, then you must not make the explanation so reasonable that the audience believes it and does not realize they are seeing an illusion nor so unreasonable that it is ludicrous, unless you are striving for comedy.

The misdirection you use must not be so subtle as to be ineffective nor so strong as to interfere with the plot you are acting out. It is possible to distract the attention of an audience by having a blank pistol fired at the rear of the auditorium, but this is so obvious an attempt to divert the eyes of the spectators away from you that it lessens their estimation of your skill.

You must fool the minds of the spectators and not their eyes. To do this you must seem to be extremely fair about letting them see what is going on. And sometimes this is more of a help than a hindrance.

Because people are most easily fooled when they think they are seeing things develop in a familiar pattern, it is often easier to fool another conjurer than it is to fool the public. All you need do to fool another conjurer is to invent a new way of doing a familiar trick. When you start to perform it, he will assume that he knows what you are going to do and therefore be more subject to misdirection than someone who had never seen the original method of doing the trick. This has had the unfortunate effect of tending to immortalize the effects created by conjurers while encouraging the invention of new methods to produce the effects.

The most fertile and unexplored field for creativity in conjuring at present is in the application of old principles to the creation of new effects. Most audiences couldn't care less what method you are using to restore a piece of rope, especially if they have seen ropes restored many times. But suppose that you brought out an electric lamp, plugged it in, turned it on, then cut the wire with insulated pliers, causing the lamp to go out, and finally brought the ends of the wire together and made a mysterious gesture over them to fuse them. The lamp suddenly goes on, the wire is restored. How? The lamp is lit by batteries, and the wire is a thin piece of rope dyed to look like electric lamp wire with a plug to go into the electric socket. The assistant who holds the lamp can turn it on and off as required and the rope is cut and restored by any of the hundreds of already carefully worked out methods. The insulated pliers would come under the heading of misdirection. There is no chance of being electrocuted by a piece of rope, but you don't want the audience to know that you are only doing one of the same old rope tricks. Changes like this, can give your performance of old tricks a new look.

Because his audience knows that the conjurer is there to fool them, it is of no use for him to make direct statements. If he picks up a deck of cards and says, "I have here an ordinary deck of cards," he will merely make the audience suspicious of the cards. It is far better to suggest that they are ordinary by handing them to someone to shuffle, spreading them out on the table to remove the joker, or in any other way suggesting that they are ordinary. If you are doing close-up conjuring and your cards are actually ordinary cards, you may casually leave them where someone who has been suspicious of them may pick them up and examine them. If they are not in fact ordinary, you might switch them for an identical looking ordinary pack and leave these out where someone can pick them up to examine them. Be sure to work out your routine, however, so you have an opportunity to switch them when attention is on something else and there is no reason for anyone to be paying close attention to the cards.

Apart from mental magic, like telepathy, prediction, or seeing without using the eyes, most conjuring consists of causing physical objects to move from one place to another in a mysterious manner. This includes vanishes, productions, transfer from one place to another, levitation, and changes of one item into another.

Levitation must be done with some sort of concealed support, devised so ingeniously that it cannot be detected by the viewer. All the others involve moving objects from view to a secret hiding place or from the secret hiding place into view. For a transfer an object is vanished in one location and either the object itself or a duplicate is produced in another location. For a change one object is vanished and another produced in the same location.

In some cases these moves between revealment and concealment can be made so rapidly by mechanical devices that the mind of the viewer cannot see the transfer. But this is difficult because the eye and mind can detect intervals of about one thirtieth of a second and this doesn't allow much time for the transfer. It also means that the hiding place must be very near the place where the apparent vanish or appearance takes place. It is much better to misdirect the audience as to the time of the vanish or appearance. For example there is a vanishing lamp trick in which the lamp collapses into the table on which it is standing. Although this trick can be startling, it is not as difficult for a spectator to see through as another trick in which a glass of water is covered with a handkerchief and then carried down near the spectators and vanished by tossing the handkerchief into the air. In this case, too, the object to be vanished goes into the table top; but the handkerchief has in it a ring that simulates the form of the glass and makes the audience think the glass is in the handkerchief long after it is actually gone. This makes the apparent vanish more of an illusion for the glass seems to melt into nothing with no nearby hiding place.

Attention can be misdirected from the secret hiding place by making it look smaller than the object that was hidden there. This can be achieved by using objects that collapse or fold up into a smaller size, as in the case of the lamp that folds up into the table. Of course the collapsible article must not be one that the audience knows to be collapsible. Producing sponge balls from an apparently empty box is not as impressive as producing cannon balls from the same box. This is why you can find such unlikely collapsible items in a conjuring shop as folding coins, plastic drinking glasses that look like glass but may be crushed, and stuffed rabbits that may be compressed to a small size. David Devant once performed a trick with a collapsible girl. He substituted a balloon in the shape of a girl for the real assistant while he seemed to be wrapping her in a large cloth. Then he carried her, or rather her balloon image wrapped in the cloth, out into the audience and opened the air valve of the balloon just as he was handing her to someone. She seemed to dissolve into nothingness in the middle of the audience.

The principles of visual illusion can often be used to direct the suspicions of the spectator away from obvious solutions to a problem. Space can be gained for hiding something by making the front edge of a table thinner than the edge away from the spectator. Thickness can further be disguised by painting the top of a table a dull dark color and putting a thin brightly colored stripe at the center of the edge to suggest that the top is really rather thin. One of the most interesting applications of this general method is a fish bowl production in which the bowl is hidden in a table top. Both the bowl and the table are apparently round but are actually oval in shape. The table, with the fish bowl concealed, is placed with its narrow end toward the audience, and when the fish bowl is produced it is placed on the table with its long side toward the audience, thereby making it look much larger than the table top and diverting suspicion from the table.

Many other illusionary principles can be used. While the mind is following a large motion, it cannot at the same time follow a small one. Therefore many sleight of hand moves that require motion of the fingers can be concealed by moving the hand while the action is going on. The mind is less apt to direct its attention to a continuous motion than to an interrupted one. If, for example, you want to switch one item for another, it is more deceptive to make the change in one continuous motion than to make it in several smaller motions. Consider the problem of exchanging a shuffled deck of cards for a prepared deck that you need for a trick. It is necessary for the cards to go out of sight, for at least a moment, to accomplish the change; the hardest part is covering up this suspicious action psychologically. One conjurer's solution was to change the cards in the act of moving a chair into position for a volunteer from the audience who was to participate in the trick. On the back of the chair was a clip holding the prepared deck and an openmouthed bag for depositing the shuffled deck. As he moved the chair, his hand went in back of it for an instant, long enough to drop one deck and pick up the other. The change was not only unseen but unsuspected by the audience because it was covered by a natural action and was accomplished without hesitation, in the course of the uninterrupted act of moving the chair.

Misdirection can not only be used to hide something that is going on from the spectator, but can be used to suggest that something is happening that is not actually happening. An object can be apparently vanished in mid-air by a performer who is a good enough mime. The performer pantomimes throwing the object in the air but actually deposits it in a secret hiding place as he brings his hand down in preparation for the throw. If the object is deposited in its hiding place smoothly enough and if the performer pantomimes the act of throwing it in the air and seeing it disappear well enough, it is difficult even for a spectator who knows what is going on to escape seeing the vanish happen in the air.

A famous psychologist once made a test of this use of suggestion and found that children were more susceptible than adults, and that girls were more susceptible than boys. When he pretended to throw a ball in the air, but actually dropped it behind his desk, he found that 60% of the girls and 40% of the boys he tried it on saw the ball disappear in the air, or thought they did. If the professor had been an expert at sleight of hand, the percentages would have been higher; but his results are of interest to conjurers because they point out one form of misdirection that works better on children than on adults. Usually children are harder to misdirect than adults. The reason for this is that the best candidates for misdirection are those who know the most and can therefore be directed along the false but apparently logical path the conjurer wants them to follow.

Preparation

ALTHOUGH the conjurer must seem to produce magical effects extemporaneously, he must often rely on careful preparation to produce those effects. Some of the best examples of this occur in those tricks where the spectator is allowed an apparently free choice.

Many card tricks, perhaps too many, start with the spectator choosing a card and end with the production of that card by the performer from some unusual place or in some unusual manner. One way of accomplishing this is to put a card in the place where it is to be discovered long before it is chosen and then to force the choice of a duplicate of that card when the trick is presented. The forced duplicate should, of course be destroyed or palmed out of the deck before the conclusion of the trick to prevent someone's noticing that there are duplicates. Sometimes the destruction of the card can be a part of the trick itself. The card planted beforehand may be in a cigarette, in a lemon, in a wallet, buried in the back yard, welded between two steel plates, frozen in a cake of ice, or put anywhere else imagination and resources can suggest.

On paper this sounds simple, but in practice you will find that carrying out this sort of trick presents a great many interesting challenges. First, the force must be very convincing. The spectator must not suspect that his choice was determined by the conjurer. This can be done by using what is known as the classic force. In this, the card to be forced is in a location known to the conjurer, the pack of cards is spread from hand to hand to allow the choice of one by the spectator. The conjurer times the rate at which he spreads the cards, keeping track of the force card, so that as the spectator reaches for a card he is almost sure to take the force card. The reason this works is that the conjurer has done it thousands of times and has developed an instinctive sense of timing in the psychological force of the card. The spectator on the other hand is doing something unfamiliar and can be led into following the path of least resistance. If the spectator, suspects that he is being led and takes the wrong card, the performer must be ready without showing the slightest sign of irritation to do some other trick that does not require the force card. He can then come back to the trick with the force card, using another spectator to select a card. Some people become so expert they can even force cards on other conjurers who know that a card is to be forced on them.

There are hundreds of other methods of forcing a card, some requiring sleight of hand and some requiring nothing but subtlety. Perhaps the least subtle is to use a deck of cards consisting of fifty-two duplicates of the card to be forced. Although infallible, this method requires more nerve to carry off than the classic force. To make it effective, the deck of duplicates must be switched for a regular deck of cards that has been used for previous tricks.

The force is only one of the details that must be worked out to suit the personality and style of the performer. The more incredible the location in which the card is to be discovered, the stronger must be the evidence that the card finally discovered is really the same one that was destroyed or vanished. Since it is not actually the same one, there is plenty of room for ingenuity in covering this weak point. The selected card may be torn into pieces and one of the pieces given to the spectator for safe keeping. When the restored card is found in its unbelievable location it is missing one corner, which fits exactly the corner held by the spectator. It must fit, because it is the original corner of the planted card. It was added to the torn pieces of the selected card by the performer and then given to the spectator as if it were one of the pieces. Even more subtle methods of identification can be used. The performer may ask a spectator for his initials and write them on the card selected. The performer neglects to let the audience know that he learned the spectator's initials before the performance and put those same initials on the planted card. The spectator may even be allowed to write his name on the card selected, if the performer has been able to get a copy of the spectator's signature in advance and has copied it on the card. In this case it is well to switch the duplicate for the original before letting the actual signer see it.

In many cases where it is necessary to force a choice

of something to produce a magical effect, advance preparation can insure that there will be no element of chance in the spectator's choice. Entire books have been printed in which the same word occurs at the same position on each page, even though the text is different on each page. For example the same word might be the first word of the ninth line on each page, so by forcing the number nine on the spectator, then having him open the book to any page and count down to the ninth line, the conjurer is sure to get the word he has already written. The number can be forced by a mathematical principle. For example if the spectator writes down a number with three digits, reverses it producing another three digit number, subtracts the smaller from the larger, and then adds the digits of the result, he will always have either 9, 18, or 27. If it is either of the latter, if he adds the digits again, he cannot escape arriving at the number 9. Any multiple of 7 can be forced by rolling dice and adding the numbers on the top and bottom of the dice. On each die the top and bottom number will add up to 7. Two dice will force 14 and three dice, 21.

If a choice is to be made from a small number of articles, the conjurer can interpret the spectator's choice to force the item he wants chosen. For example if you want to force one of three items, lay them down in line with the force one in the center. Ask the spectator to point to one, and he will usually choose the center one because it is the easiest one to specify. If he does, you have the one you want. If he chooses one of the others, discard it and ask him to pick up one of the remaining two. If he now picks up the force one, discard the other. If he picks up the other non force item tell him to discard it. Notice that you must be very careful of your language in order to control the spectator. In the first instance you asked him to point to one, not to choose one. This enables you to interpret his pointing as you choose, either to keep the one he points to or to discard it. In the second instance you tell him to pick up one of the two. You still haven't told him what you intend to do, and have not even implied that he is choosing one by picking it up, so you can interpret his picking it up to suit yourself. This sort of a force must be done smoothly and confidently, not putting any special emphasis on what is being done. The conjurer must act as if he really doesn't care which item is chosen and is merely being very fair about allowing the spectator a free choice.

Careful preparation can not only be used to force a choice on a spectator, but it can be used to remove the necessity of forcing. You can have a different conclusion prepared for each of the possible choices that the spectator might make. This is really a variation of the method used in the above force of one of three items. You allow a free choice and then interpret it to suit your own purposes. As an extreme example, let us say you have hidden duplicates of all fifty-two cards in your deck in different locations. You can now allow a perfectly free choice of one of the cards in the deck, destroy it, and have it found reincarnated in some unlikely location. Not having told the audience what you intended to do, they have no way of knowing that the ending would have been different for each one of the cards in the deck. One would not often do this much preparation, but the principle is useful, especially in mental tricks of prediction and divination.

Acting

THE CONJURING performer must be an actor, but a very specialized sort of actor. Conjuring requires acting that is deep rather than wide. The conjurer need not play many different roles. Instead he must create one character and play that character all during his career, altering the playlets in which he performs his miracles to suit the character rather than playing a new part in each playlet.

It is possible to perform conjuring without using the voice, but it is not possible to perform conjuring without using gestures and postures of the body. Sleight of hand is really a highly developed form of pantomime. A pure mime, like Marcel Marceau, uses his body to pantomime actions that can be understood by the audience because they are possible actions. A pure conjurer, like Cardini, uses his body and a minimum of properties to pantomime actions that are impossible, although clearly seen by the audience. Marceau's pantomime transmits emotions like joy, sorrow, and fear to the audience. Cardini's pantomime transmits emo-

161

tions like wonder, amazement, and laughter.

Pantomime is useful to the conjurer in three different ways. It is useful in creating the character the conjurer is playing. It is useful in acting out the plot of the magical effect being produced. It is useful in disguising secret actions that may be necessary to achieve the effect. Many of the greatest conjurers have found that their performances were most effective in pantomime without words. Among them have been Chung Ling Soo, Okito, Cardini, and Channing Pollock.

Other great conjurers have found it desirable to talk to their audiences, but to keep the number of words as few as possible. It is difficult for a spectator to give his full attention to two things at the same time. If he is listening, he is not looking as carefully as he might be, and he may not be watching closely enough to be properly impressed by the climax of the trick. Words are used to impart necessary information to the audience and to misdirect the audience's attention when necessary. It generally pays a performer to learn to speak well, and to speak in a manner fitting the character he is playing.

The technique of acting, whether of pantomime or voice, cannot be learned from books. It must be learned from a good teacher or by actual experience before audiences or in both ways. Most actors either study dramatics formally or begin by acting small parts with other more experienced people carrying the main burden of the play. Most conjurers on the other hand start out performing small tricks for their friends and relatives, then branch out to performing at parties, church affairs, lodges, and banquets, and finally, perhaps, become semi-professionals or even, in rare cases, professionals. Not only are they self-taught but many of them have never even worked with a more experienced performer. Although often clever at the technical aspects of conjuring, they are often criticized for their poor acting ability. Considering how they were trained, the most miraculous thing is that they can act at all.

In doing close-up tricks for friends, a natural style is best, and dramatic training is not only not needed but may be harmful. It is easy to tell if a friend is being natural or is acting. The close-up performer requires a high degree of technical skill and a good personality. It is when one performs in public for large groups that one needs training in the arts of the theater. If formal training is impossible, he should try to work with a good conjurer as an assistant. Some of the greatest of conjurers learned their craft this way, notably Chung Ling Soo, Harry Kellar, and Fred Keating. Unfortunately at present there are very few large shows that require assistants. Many professional conjurers give lessons, and on the west coast there is a school for conjurers. If you do not have an opportunity for any of these then you will have to learn by observing the best conjurers and practicing on audiences wherever you can find them. In any case, if you learn from another conjurer, be very careful that you do not end up doing his act. It is all too easy to learn someone else's act rather than his craft.

However you learn the acting craft, you will have to create a character to portray in your performances. This character may be only a slight modification of your offstage character, as in the case of Alexander Herrmann, or it may be entirely different from your offstage self, as in the case of Cardini. But it must be a distinctive character that is instantly recognizable as your performing self. In order to make your conjuring interesting, you must make the character you are acting as a magician an interesting one, and it must be different from any other performer if you are to have any hope of success. You may choose the character as you please, subject only to your own limitations, but once you have chosen you must live within the bounds you have chosen. Very few actors in other areas have this opportunity to create their own character. In working it out you should take advantage of all your own strengths and even your weaknesses. You may find out that they are not really weaknesses at all. If you look suave and handsome, you may want to do a graceful act of manipulative magic. If you have an oversize nose or some other odd physical feature, you can play comedy. If you speak with a foreign accent, you can use it to attract attention to what you say and improve your misdirection. If you are very strong and wiry, you may want to do escape magic. Almost any characteristic, physical or mental, can be used to advantage in creating a conjuring personality that you can play. Okito's great-grandfather became a magician because he had a wooden leg and it came in handy for hiding production items.

There is one thing of which you must be careful. A conjurer creates illusions for others to enjoy, but he must himself be a realist in order to create illusion. If he starts to believe in illusion himself, he is lost. If you are short, fat, and not handsome, you will never become a tall, thin, suave matinee idol type of magician. You can become a great magician, but you must create an onstage self that uses all your abilities and characteristics.

Dexterity

To be proficient as a conjurer, one must have a knowledge of the principles and methods of deception, the ability to act in front of an audience, and dexterity. Many books have been written stressing the idea that conjuring is fun, conjuring is easy, you can perform miracles without skill, etc. It is true, you can purchase apparatus that will produce deceptive effects without requiring much skill on your part; and you can find many simple tricks that can be performed with little skill. You can also become an instant piano player by putting on a record of Van Cliburn playing a piano concerto. But you must not expect audiences to gasp with admiration and applaud your talent. Audiences are very intelligent, and they will know whether or not you possess skill.

To some extent it is possible to substitute skill in acting for skill with the hands and mind, but a truly clumsy conjurer is very rare. On the other hand it is also possible to some extent to substitute skill with the hands for skill in acting, but this makes the conjurer into a sort of juggler and removes much of the charm and interest that conjuring can possess.

Like an iceberg, the skill of the conjurer must be nine-tenths submerged. The conjurer is supposed to act the part of a person who can do mysterious things, or to whom miraculous things happen; if he makes too much of a display of his skill, he destroys some of the mystery. On the other hand, no audience likes to think it is being entertained by someone without skill, so many conjurers have found it desirable to include some open demonstrations of skill in their performances. It is usually also wise to intermingle in the same perform-ance feats performed purely by concealed skill, feats that rely entirely on some concealed and subtle prin-ciple, and feats performed by means of apparatus. This makes it easier to catch the spectators off guard, since they are likely to be looking for dexterous moves in an apparatus trick and trying to puzzle out the workings of some sort of secret apparatus when the conjurer isn't using any.

The development of dexterity is also important be-cause of its effect on the performer. It might be pos-sible to use ingenious apparatus that would convince the audience that the performer was skillful, but the performer himself would know better and the knowl-edge would corrode his soul. The best way to be happy is to exercise some skill that you have worked hard to develop. The best way to be unhappy is to seek pres-tige based on falsehood.

Hands are so important to man in general that more of the cortex of the brain is devoted to the hands than to all the rest of the body from the neck down. The hands and what they can do are so important to a conjurer that Robert-Houdin once said that there were three things necessary to a conjurer: first, dexterity; second, dexterity; and third, dexterity. It is no coincidence that so many of the words used to describe conjuring refer to the hands: sleight of hand, prestidigitation (quickness of the fingers), and legerdemain (lightness of hand). No one, of course, can move his hands, fingers, or any other part of the body so rapidly as to deceive another person. The skill of the conjurer is in performing secret actions with the hands while at the same time making natural gestures.

After thousands of years of sleight of hand one might think that all the possible sleight of hand moves had been invented long ago, but this is not at all true. Anyone who reads current conjuring literature sees an unending flood of new moves described by enthusiastic inventors. Conjuring is a very individualistic art. There are many basic moves and many classic and standard tricks, but each good conjurer finds his own way of accomplishing them and using them because each conjurer is an individual and has his own individual abilities and limitations.

There are certain limitations of the hands that apply to everyone. The joint in the wrist does not rotate, if you want to turn your hand over you must move your forearm. If you place your hand, palm down, flat on a table and try to raise each of your fingers individually from the table, you will find that they can all be raised easily except the third finger, the one next to the little finger. If the fingers are kept straight but bent at right angles to the palm at the first knuckle you will find that you cannot spread them apart. But apart from this, each individual is different and has hands with fingers of different length, of varying strength, with "windows" between the fingers because of large knuckles and thin fingers, with short pudgy fingers, or with or without fleshy pads at the tips of the fingers. Each individual must work out his own minor variations on standard sleight of hand moves and invent new moves that he can perform better than other people because of his own individual peculiarities.

Decorative Sleights

THERE ARE many decorative sleights or flourishes with coins and cards that may be practiced to develop the type of dexterity required in conjuring. These flourishes are also of use in a performance to impress the audience with the fact that the performer possesses skill. Whether they should be used in a particular performer's routine or not depends on the character the performer is portraying. They should not be dragged in by the heels just to show that the performer is clever. The conjurer must convince his audience that he has talent without convincing them that he is a showoff.

In any case the ability to perform some of these flourishes is a useful accomplishment and an aid to learning the more difficult sleight of hand moves that must be done without being visible to the audience.

THE COIN ROLL

The coin roll is a flourish in which a coin is made to rotate, spinning, around and around the hand with a minimum of motion of the hand and fingers. If done well the coin seems to be spinning around almost by its own free will. The necessary moves are illustrated in figs. A-1 to A-8. The coin is first held between the thumb and first finger as far back toward the knuckles as you can manage, then pushed over the first finger by the thumb and allowed to rotate over the first finger until it is caught on the opposite edge by pinching it lightly between the first and second fingers. By tightening the grip of the first and second fingers the coin is rotated farther until it is upright and by slightly raising the first finger the coin is tipped over and allowed to fall over the second finger whereupon it is caught between the second and third fingers. The same process is repeated to roll the coin over the second finger and again over the third finger where it is allowed to fall through the space between the third and little fingers, guided by the little finger, from where it is picked up by the thumb which has moved over to the little finger under the hand and carried by the thumb back to the starting position. The entire move must be done with the fingers closed into a fist, or as near to a fist as you can manage. If the fingers stick out too much they waggle up and down and destroy the impression that the coin is almost flying around the hand by itself. When you first begin to practice, the coin will limp around instead of flying; but if you select a coin suited to the size of your hand and practice long enough, you will get the feel of the manipulation. The coin that suits most people is a half dollar; and when you have learned to perform the manipulation, it looks best when the back of the hand is toward the spectators, as in fig. A-9. After you develop enough

A 1

A 2

A 3

A 4

A 5

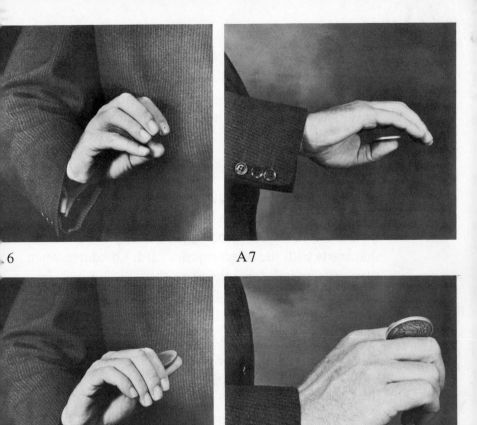

6   A7

8   A9

COIN ROLL

skill to perform this with one coin, you can practice with two coins at the same time, or with one coin traveling around both hands, by holding one hand above the other.

CARD FAN

The object of this manipulation is to spread the cards neatly in the hands, for the purpose of displaying them or to allow someone to pick one for a card trick that starts with the selection of a card. Of course when they are spread for selection, they are spread face down. They are fanned face up to prove that all the cards are different. With cards that have a back design that runs all the way out to the edge of the cards, that is with no white border, attractive designs may be formed by fanning the cards with the backs toward the audience. The design can be changed by reversing the cards end for end, if the back design is not symmetrical. Some conjurers have built up entire routines of card fans.

Not all cards fan equally well. To form a good fan, as in fig. B-4, the cards must be reasonably new and clean. Some brands and types of cards fan better than others. Often the cheapest are the best, and the worst are the expensive ones with gold edges. If the cards you want to use do not fan evenly, you can coat them with a fanning powder, obtainable from magic dealers. In an emergency you can use good baby powder from the drug store. Put some of the powder on a piece of cotton and rub it all over the two faces of each card, and the cards will slip over each other more smoothly.

To make the simplest form of fan, the cards are held as shown in fig. B-1, deep in the crotch of the left

CARD FAN

thumb. The cards are held between the tip of the thumb and the side of the first finger. The closer to the lower left hand corner of the cards the pressure point is, the larger the resulting fan will be. Smaller fans can be made by moving the pressure point closer to the center of the deck. The right hand is then brought over the cards as in fig. B-2, with the tip of the right first finger resting against the upper left edge of the pack of cards. The right hand is then rotated in a clockwise direction as the right first finger guides the cards into the fan as shown in figs. B-3 and B-4.

CARD SPREAD AND TURNOVER

This flourish is used for very much the same purposes as the fan, except that it is performed on a table or other surface instead of in the hands. It may be used to show the spectators the deck of cards or to spread them out so someone can select one. It has also been used for comedy. By starting a card trick with a very rapid spread of the cards on the table, flipping them over, and immediately scooping them up, while saying, "Now that you have examined the cards,——" a slight, if skeptical, smile may sometimes be brought to the face of a spectator. Sensing his doubt, you may then hand him the cards to examine, providing they are the kind that will stand examination.

To perform this sleight, you must learn to riffle the cards with one hand. This is done by holding the deck with the thumb at one end and the second and third fingers at the other end, with the first fingertip pressing down on the exact center of the back of the deck. If the deck is held in this way while it rests on the other hand, or the table, and the thumb and the second and

Card Spread and Turnover

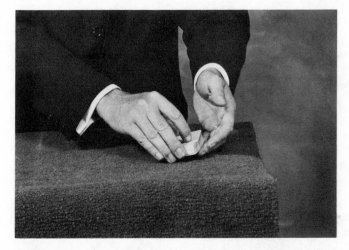

C 1

2

C 3

C 4

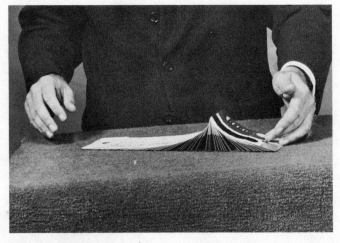

C 5

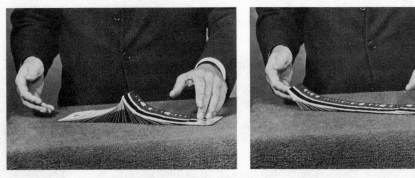

C 6   C 7

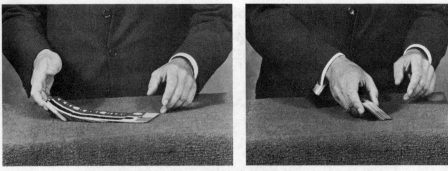

C 8   C 9

third fingers are drawn upward while the first finger holds the deck down at the center, the cards will be dropped down one by one in rapid sequence. The cards are held down in the center and bowed upward by lifting their ends with the second and third finger and the thumb, and are released in a steady stream controlled by the sense of touch of the first and second finger and the thumb. The first finger merely exerts enough pressure to hold the center down.

If you riffle the cards in this way while moving your hand across the table, you will find that you can spread the cards out in a line and they will be evenly spaced if you riffled them at a steady pace and moved your hand at a steady pace across the table.

If you start the spread with the left fingertips under the edge of the deck as in fig. C-1 and spread the cards while riffling them, as in figs. C-2 and C-3, you will be in position to turn the spread over by pressing on the end card as in fig. C-4. The speed with which the spread of cards turn over can be controlled by the pressure you exert on the end card, figs. C-5 and C-6. When doing this you will find that it is even possible to make the turnover of the cards stop and then begin again merely by the pressure you exert on the end card. When the turnover reaches the other end of the spread, the right hand is used to catch the last card as it turns over as shown in fig. C-7 and the right hand then scoops the cards up as shown in figs. C-8 and C-9.

ONE-HANDED CUT

In the language of conjuring, dividing a deck of cards into two or more packets of cards and transposing them is called a cut. Only seeming to do this is called a false cut. Actually cutting the deck without letting the audience see that it has been cut is called a pass. The one-handed cut described below could also be called a one-handed pass because it is sometimes used as a means of secretly cutting the cards.

This sleight is best performed with bridge width cards. In addition to some rather bizarre extra large and extra small sizes, playing cards come in two widths, usually known as poker width and bridge width. Unless you have extraordinarily long fingers, you will find this sleight much easier with bridge size cards.

The cards are held well down in the hand, as shown in fig. D-1, the bottom edge of the deck farthest from the wrist touching the second and third fingers at the outer finger joints. The thumb reaches over the deck and lifts off some of the cards, as shown in fig. D-2, while the forefinger and the little finger are pulled back under the deck; the lower half of the deck is gripped between the tips of the second and third fingers and the backs of the finger nails of the first and little fingers. The thumb pulls the upper half of the deck back as far as it can. Then the lower packet of cards, held in a vise between the first and little finger underneath the ends of the packet and the second and third fingers at the center above, is moved out from under the top of the deck by extending the fingers out until the edge of the lower packet clears the edge of the packet held by the thumb, fig. D-3.

The thumb then drops its packet onto the hand, the fingers close enough to bring what was originally the lower packet over the packet now lying on the hand, and the packet held by the fingers is dropped onto the

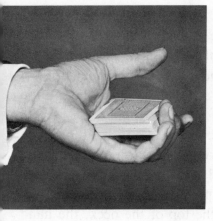

1

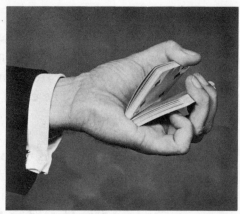

D2

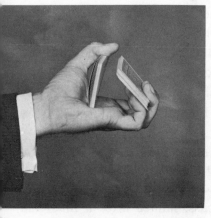

D4

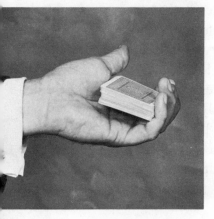

REVERSE CHARLIER PASS

packet on the hand. The pack is gripped by the base of the thumb enough to allow the first and little fingers to be withdrawn from under the deck without disturbing the cards. The cards are now cut and lying on the hand, fig. D-5.

In order to use this cut as a flourish, it must be practiced until it is done easily and smoothly, with no evidence of struggle while it is being done. If it is to be used as a secret manipulation to cut the cards and bring a desired card to the top of the deck, the hand must be screened from sight, at least momentarily while the cut is made. This can be done while covering the deck with a handkerchief, or by reaching for something with the hand that is not holding the cards in such a way that the arm crosses over the hand holding the cards and momentarily hides the cards. Or in any of a number of ways you may devise.

ONE-HANDED CUT (CHARLIER)

This move is similar to the previous one except that it is done in the reverse direction. It is sometimes known as the Charlier pass, named after a magician called Charlier, who was so mysterious that very little is known about him except that he was one of the cleverest card manipulators of all time. He used to turn up at irregular intervals in different cities, always ragged but wearing a top hat, and give lessons in sleight of hand and performances for private parties. He disappeared as mysteriously as he lived, and no one knows what happened to him.

The sleight is performed by holding the cards at the finger tips, between the tip of the thumb and the outer joints of the second and third fingers as shown in fig.

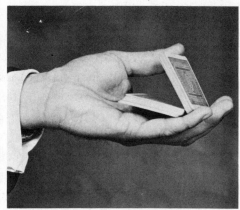

1

E 2

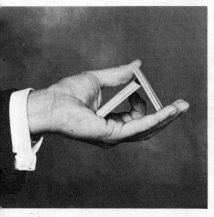

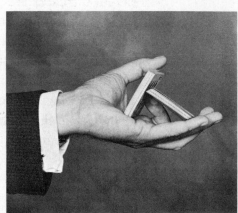

3

E 4

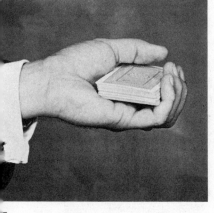

5

CHARLIER PASS

E-1. The first finger is used to steady the deck at the outer end. The thumb allows some of the cards to drop down onto the hand, fig. E-2, and the first finger moves back and presses on the face of this dropped packet fig. E-3. The first finger continues to press upward on this packet until the edge of it clears the edge of the packet still held between the thumb and finger tips, fig. E-4. The first finger is then quickly withdrawn, the thumb releases its hold, and the two packets drop into the hand fig. E-5. The deck has been cut. Because in this sleight the cards are not gripped between opposing fingers, the hand must be held in such a position that the cards do not slide off the hand and onto the floor. If they slide a little out of alignment in performing the sleight, they can be straightened after performing the sleight by tapping the outer end of the deck with the first finger while the thumb and the other three fingers hold the deck securely.

Sleight of Hand

A REAL magician could presumably cause objects to appear and disappear at will. Not being real magicians, conjurers can only cause objects to disappear by hiding them somewhere. To make something disappear you must first show it to the spectator long enough to establish its existence in his mind. Beginners sometimes make the mistake of vanishing something so fast that the spectators don't really realize it was there to begin with. Having established the existence of the thing that is to be vanished, you then proceed to transfer it to a secret hiding place, disguising the time, the place, and the means of transfer by any means, mechanical, optical, and psychological that can be devised. The simplest illustrations of this are to be found in pure sleight of hand.

The most common secret action to be performed is the concealment of objects by the hands. This is called palming by conjurers, whether the palm of the hand is used or not. If the object is concealed by the fingers, it is said to be finger palmed. If it is held by the thumb, it is said to be thumb palmed. If it is held on the back of the hand, it is back palmed. If it is concealed by the wrist, it is rear palmed. Much of the art of sleight of hand consists of transferring articles to or from the palmed position while pantomiming some action that is intended to be seen by the spectator. For example a coin may be palmed in the right hand while it is apparently being placed in the left hand by the right hand. Cards may be back palmed while pantomime leads the audience to believe they are being thrown into the air. A ball may be palmed while it is apparently being placed under a cup.

Palming is so fundamental to sleight of hand that it must be practiced until it becomes second nature to the conjurer. It must be worked at until objects can be retained in the hand as long as required without the hand showing any unnatural stiffness or awkwardness. The hand must be relaxed so it can perform other actions without betraying the presence of the palmed object. It should not be necessary to think about the palmed object or the hand, nor should it be necessary to think about keeping the hand in the proper position so the palmed object is not visible to the spectator. Many aspiring conjurers have made it a habit to keep a coin or other object palmed in the hand almost constantly to teach themselves to palm without having to think about it. In fact one of the authors has a silver dollar in his palm while he is typing this manuscript.

To find the correct position for the ordinary coin palm, look at the palm of your hand as you alternately tighten and relax the muscles. You will observe a mound of flesh that runs from the base of the little finger back to the wrist and another that runs around the base of the thumb and back to the wrist. It is between these two mounds that the coin must be held. If you hold a coin balanced on the tips of the two middle fingers, the back of the hand up and the fingers bent, and then press the coin into the palm with the two middle fingers, it will land in the palm in the correct position to be held by a contraction of the muscles of the hand. This will be difficult at first, but with practice it is possible to hold not only one but a number of coins in the palm this way and even release them one by one by relaxing the muscle at the base of the thumb.

With the coin or coins held in this manner, the hand must look perfectly natural to a spectator. The usual error made by a beginner is to attempt to hold the fingers straight and extended, which causes the thumb to stick out as if it were hitchhiking a ride. This is not the normal position of the human hand at rest. Look at the hands of other people when they are at rest. Your hand holding a palmed object should look no different from those of other people when they are relaxed.

In a scientific study made in connection with piano playing technique, it was found that 87% of all hands at rest assume a position with the fingers flexed, the amount of flexion increasing from the index finger to the little finger. Only 1% of all hands at rest assume a position with all the fingers held straight. It is wise then for a conjurer to learn to hold his hands in the position used by the great majority of people.

After learning to hold a coin in this way, you can go on to learning to place the coin in the palmed position while you are pantomiming the act of placing it in the left hand. Look in a mirror and see what happens when you really place a coin in the left hand. Then go through the same motions, but palm the coin in the right hand. The real action and the false one must look absolutely identical.

PALMING A COIN

The coin is held between the thumb and first finger of the right hand as in fig. G-1 and displayed to the spectator. The right hand is then brought toward the left hand, which is opened and brought into the position shown in fig. G-1 after the motion of the right hand toward the left begins. The major motion must be with the right hand, because you are trying to create the impression that the coin is being placed in the left hand by the right hand. The right hand is brought into contact with the left hand, and the thumb of the left hand passes through the space between the thumb and first finger of the right hand. The coin is now surrounded by the thumb and fingers of the left hand, fig. G-2. The left hand now moves forward as if it were taking the coin, but instead the coin is dropped into the fingers of the right hand, fig. G-3. The left hand is now closed tightly, as if it were clutching the coin and is moved away from the right hand. The right hand, having apparently finished what it was doing is now moved less than the left hand; it is relaxed and is used to point to the left hand, fig. G-4. During this entire transfer, the placing of a coin in the left hand must be pantomimed with the hands, the eyes, and the entire body. You must almost convince yourself that you have really placed a coin in the left hand. The eyes must follow the supposed placing of the coin. The entire attention must be

G 1

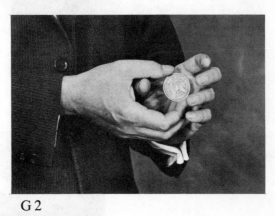

G 2

G 3

COIN VANISHING

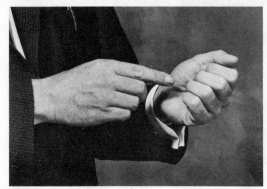

G 4

G 5

G 6

G 7

shifted from the right hand to the left hand when the coin is apparently transferred from the right hand to the left.

You now have possession of the coin in the right hand as shown in fig. G-5, which shows the situation as seen from the performer's viewpoint, the spectators of course are on the other side. But this is a view, even the performer should never see, except when reading a description of how to perform the sleight. When you are hiding something, never look at the hiding place because your eyes will draw attention to it. The coin is now in a finger palmed position. It can be readily transferred to the ordinary palm position by pressing it into position with the tips of the second and third fingers fig. G-6. This can only be done however when the hand is in motion. Moving the fingers even a little will call attention to the hand unless the hand is at the same time making a gesture, picking up something, or for any other reason is in motion. When the coin is properly held in the ordinary palm position, fig. G-7, the hand may be held and used normally although its back must always be kept toward the spectators.

You now have a situation in which your audience thinks you are holding a coin in the closed left hand (that is if you pantomimed your part well), whereas you really have a coin held in your relaxed right hand. Before you show that the coin has vanished from the left hand it is well to dispose of the coin in the right hand so you will be able to show that too. Since attention is now on the hand that is supposed to be holding the coin it is not too difficult to get rid of the coin in the act of picking something up or by devising some excuse for the right hand to be out of view for a moment. Native magicians in India use a bag to carry their properties and they keep the bag on the ground next to them while they perform. In reaching into the bag to get items they also dispose of such un-wanted items as the coin palmed in the right hand. European magicians used to use an apron that was called a gibeciere for the same purpose. Much more recently a performer on television simply lowered his hand out of the frame of the picture and dropped the coin on the floor. If you should try this, be sure that either the floor is carpeted or the sound man turns down the sound when the coin hits the floor. You might even create a very simple trick by first palming the coin as above, keeping the audience's attention on your left hand while you tug your left coat sleeve back a little with your right hand, bringing the palmed coin over the opening of your handkerchief pocket on the left side of your suit coat and dropping the coin in this pocket. Then when you open your left hand to show that the coin has vanished, you can also open your right hand, providing you have moved it away from the pocket early enough to prevent attracting attention to the closeness of the hand to the pocket. To carry the trick one step farther you might have your tailor extend the handkerchief pocket with a tube of cloth, the seams on the upper side, diagonally around the inside of your coat to connect with the right hand coat pocket. Then you could have the coin marked for identification, palm it in placing it in the left hand, drop it in the upper pocket when tugging the sleeve back, show that the coin has vanished from the left hand, show the right hand empty, and ask someone to reach in your right coat pocket where he will find the marked coin. Since your hands never came near the right hand pocket, this leaves the audience with something to puzzle over. They are not likely to suspect the coat for two reasons. First it is a normal item that does not attract suspicion because it does not look like magic apparatus. Secondly, people tend not to realize that anyone would go to all that trouble in order to perform what looks like an extemporaneous trick. However even this very simple trick, as you can see, requires dexterity, preparation, misdirection, and skill in pantomime.

You can also see how, after learning some of the fundamental principles and skills, you can devise all sorts of variations and combinations to form new tricks. By now you can probably think of other ways to get rid of the palmed coin. Or perhaps you would rather not use a coin. You can borrow a ring from someone and use it for a similar trick. It might even be good misdirection to have the spectator tie a handkerchief around your clenched left hand to prevent the ring escaping. Inventing new ways to use even one simple trick can offer endless hours of pleasure.

Card Sleights

THE HISTORY of conjuring goes back thousands of years and playing cards have been with us only hundreds of years, so they are relatively newcomers to the conjuring scene; but more sleight of hand moves and more tricks have been invented for playing cards than for any other single class of objects used in conjuring. The reason for this is that cards are not only of a convenient size to handle, but they may be used in many different ways. They can be used as objects to produce and vanish and can be used as objects to be identified. They can be used for mental tricks and for flourishes. They can be used for mathematical tricks and for tricks accomplished by pure sleight of hand. They can be used for tricks based on color changes of faces or backs and they can be used for demonstrations of gambling tricks. The possibilities are almost infinite.

Most of the card tricks based on mathematical principles and those that involve the finding of a chosen card by means of more or less subtle principles are banal and uninteresting. They appeal only to the

194

person who is doing the trick and to the minority of people who like to solve puzzles. In order to be really interesting as entertainment, a card trick must be so spectacular in effect that even the least acute spectator is aware that a near miracle has occurred. To do this requires skill and inventiveness. To develop skill there is no better way than to jump right in and start with one of the oldest but still the most generally useful sleights in all card conjuring, the two-handed pass. Because it is difficult to perform indetectably many substitutes for it have been invented, but even the substitutes can be better learned and used if one also knows how to perform the two-handed pass.

TWO-HANDED PASS

From the spectator's viewpoint this move looks like the sequence shown in illustrations H-1, H-2, and H-3, which show the hands performing the two handed pass from the spectators' side. This does not look very impressive and it is not intended to. What has happened is that the deck has been cut without the spectator's realizing it. This may sound like a small thing, but it makes many more impressive things possible. A card in the center of the deck may be brought to the top or bottom, a cut made by a spectator may be neutralized, the cards in the center of the deck may be interchanged with those on the top and bottom, and a card selected by a spectator may be placed under the control of the conjurer. The ability to do these things frees the ingenuity of the conjurer and allows him to invent many different effects with cards.

The first step is to secure a small break in the deck of cards at the point where the cut is to be made.

When a selected card is returned to the deck the tip of the left little finger is put in contact with the face of the card while the cards are spread for the return of the card. When the deck is squared up, the little finger is kept in contact with the card, but is slid back to the near right corner of the deck, fig. H-4, maintaining a slight break in the deck. This puts the selected card at the bottom of the upper of two packets of cards, and when the pass is made the selected card will be at the bottom of the deck. If it is desired to bring the selected card to the top, the little finger must initially be placed in contact with the face of the card above the selected card. Note that if this break is formed correctly, it is invisible from the viewpoint of the spectator, fig. H-5. It is invisible because there is no break at the end of the deck toward the spectator, only at the end of the deck toward the performer.

The right hand is brought over the deck, apparently to square-up the deck. The right hand grips the deck at the extreme left edge, first finger at the outer end and thumb at the inner end, fig. H-6. Illustrations H-6 to H-9 show the following procedure but with the right arm raised to allow the move to be seen clearly. First the left little finger is inserted farther into the break at the rear of the deck, still preventing the formation of a break at the front end of the deck by pressing down with the tip of the second finger. The top packet is then moved down and to the right, held between the outside of the little finger of the left hand and the inside of the second and third finger tips opposite. At the same time the right hand edge of the lower packet is moved upward by exerting pressure downward with the left thumb and shifting the

Two Hand Pass

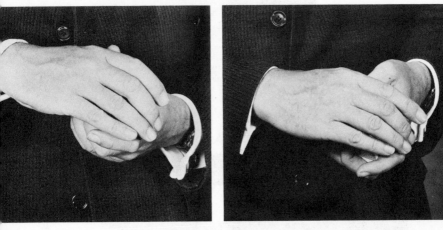

H1   H2

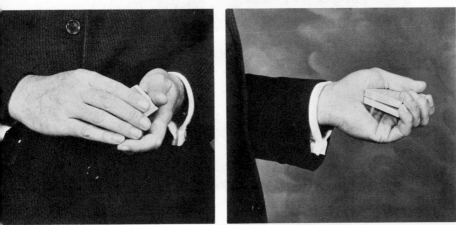

H3   H4

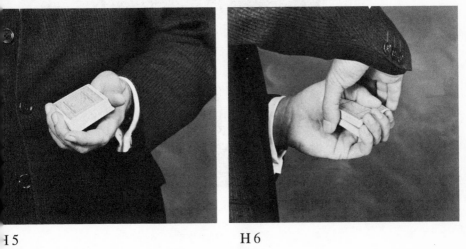

H5   H6

H 7

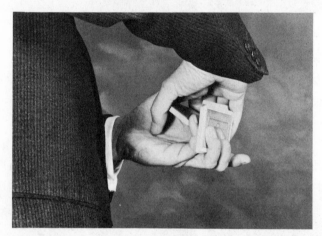

H 8

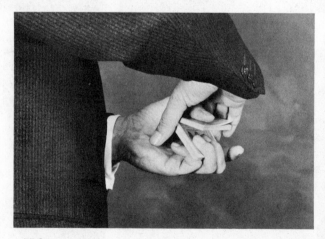

H 9

grip at the outer end to the right second finger, figs. H-7 and H-8. These moves will allow the right edge of the lower packet to clear the left edge of the upper packet. The left fingers then close, bringing the original top packet under the original bottom packet, fig. H-9. At this point the right hand begins to slide over to the right, actually squaring the cards by running the thumb along the inner end and the second finger along the outer end of the deck. The entire operation must be screened as well as possible by the fingers of the right hand, which must be moved as little as possible.

All this takes a long time to describe but when it is well practiced it can be done in a fraction of a second. The exact methods of accomplishing the sleight are often modified, because each person's hands are different. You may have to work out a variation of your own, keeping in mind that the object is to cut the cards while momentarily screening them from view with the right hand. Since the move is difficult to do so perfectly that it is completely invisible, you should use every device of misdirection possible to take attention away from the hands while doing it. Max Malini, a noted conjurer who was long on talent but short in stature, had such small hands that he could not do the pass invisibly. When someone asked him how he did it without being detected, he said that he waited until the spectator's eyes were not on his hands. When asked how long he would wait for this he shrugged and said "about a week."

PALMING A CARD

It is often desirable to remove a card or cards from

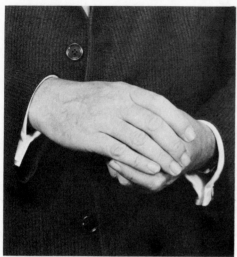 

J 1   CARD PALMING   J

the deck by palming them. This may be necessary to
remove fake cards or duplicates from the deck, to
secure possession of a wanted card for reappearance
later, or to secure a batch of cards for production in
a manipulative routine. To palm cards from the deck
with the right hand when the deck is held in the left
hand, the right hand is brought over the deck as if
to square the cards, but is never placed flat down on
the deck. A break is held under the cards to be palmed,
as in figs. H-4 and H-5. When the right hand comes
over the deck, the left little finger pushes the right
near corner of the cards to be palmed to the right
and forward, pressing the right corner of the cards
against the tip of the right little finger, bowing the cards
and pressing them into the right palm, figs. J-1 and J-2.
As in palming coins, the cards must be held in the palm
with the hand in a natural posture. Keep the thumb
close to the first finger.

Cups and Balls

IN AMERICA and Europe the cups and balls trick is usually performed with metal cups of the general design of those shown in fig. K-1, and with balls made of cork or rubber or knitted wool. These may be obtained at conjuring shops, or the trick may be done with paper cups, opaque glasses, goblets, or any other similar containers. Some of these are more suitable than others because some moves with the cups require that when the cups are stacked there be enough space between the bottoms of the cups to hide a ball. This is the reason for the ridge near the base of the cups shown. Also conjuring shop cups have a bottom surface which is concave when the cup is upside down. This allows a ball to be placed on the bottom of the cup without rolling off.

The balls are made of a material like cork or rubber so that they will not betray their presence by noise when they are being manipulated.

The three most important moves in the cups and balls are the palming of a ball together with its subsequent apparent disappearance, the apparent placing of a ball under a cup while retaining it, and the actual placing of a ball under a cup while apparently merely setting the cup down.

The balls may be palmed in many different ways, but for simplicity we will here use only the finger palm. Balls may be finger palmed in much the same way as a coin is palmed, figs. K-2 to K-6. By following the method described earlier for palming a coin, you should have no trouble in palming a ball.

The ball may be apparently placed under a cup by first palming it into the right hand as you appear to pass it to the left hand, and then pretending to place the nonexistent ball in the left hand under the cup, which is raised by the right hand. As in all sleight of hand you can study this by actually placing a ball in your left hand, picking up a cup with the right hand and placing the ball under the cup with the left hand as the right hand sets the cup down. Watch this in a mirror, and then make the action of placing the nonexistent ball in the left hand under the cup, held by the hand containing the ball palmed, look exactly the same. It is also possible to palm the ball in the very act of placing it under a cup. To do this, hold the ball between the thumb and first finger and pantomime placing it under a cup, which you lift with the left hand while you actually roll the ball with your thumb to the finger palm position.

To actually place a ball under a cup while you set a cup down, without letting the spectator know that you are doing anything but set a cup down, pick up the cup with the hand in which the ball is finger palmed, as shown from the rear in fig. K-7, and from the spec-

CUPS AND BALLS

K 1

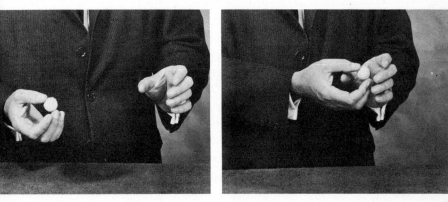

K 2

K 3

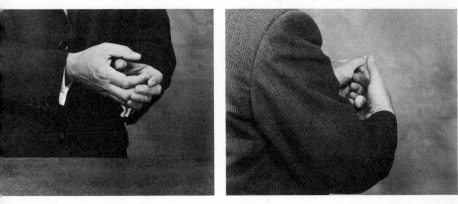

K 4

K 5

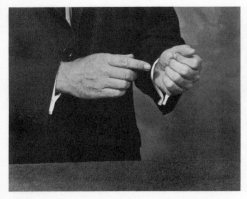

K 6

K 7

K 8

K 9

K 10

K 11

12

K13

14

K15

16

K17

tator's viewpoint in fig. K-8. Then as you set down the cup, either drop the ball so that it lands under the cup or first tilt the cup toward the spectator, dropping the ball into the cup, and then set the cup down so that the ball stays in the cup. You will find that either of these moves requires a certain rhythm of action that is hard to describe but easy to discover by playing the cups and a ball. A ball may also be placed under a cup in the act of tipping a cup toward the audience to dump a ball previously placed on the bottom of a cup into the hand, fig. K-9.

A ball may be concealed in the three cups, never leave the cup and still apparently not be there, as shown in figs. K-10 to K-14. Start with the cups stacked, bottom up. The cups are held in the hands as in fig. K-10 and then placed on the table one by one, stacking them as they are put down. By doing this with a rhythmic slightly swinging motion, the ball will not fall out of the second cup when it is put on top of the first and will hence remain in the same position it was to start with, between the bottom and center cup. Practice this at first starting with the cups mouth up, and then gradually learn to do it with the initial position almost horizontal. You will find that a slight swinging motion keeps the ball in the cup as it is moved out and placed down on the previous cup. After demonstrating in this way several times that the cups are apparently empty, the ball may be produced after placing the cups down in the same manner, but not stacked. Placing the cups in a row will put the ball under the center cup, although the audience should think that there could not be anything in any of the cups. This is called the "galloping post" move.

One cup may be apparently passed through another by dropping one cup into the other and letting the concussion of the upper one striking the lower drive the lower one out of the hand while the hand catches the upper one. To do this hold the cup lightly, as in fig. K-15 between the thumb and second finger, drop the upper cup as in fig. K-16, driving the lower cup out of the hand and catching it with the other hand as in fig. K-17.

By combining these moves an interesting routine may be created.

You will need a table with a surface that will not encourage the balls to roll off. A tablecloth can be used, and this will also be handy for holding the balls before they are mysteriously produced. On the side of the table away from the audience you can make what is called a *servante* by pinning the cloth to form a fold that will hold the balls. This should be out of sight of the audience but within easy reach of your hand. You will also need three cups, four small balls, and three larger balls or three small potatoes or anything else that is larger than the small balls but will fit easily in the cups. Stack the cups with one small ball between the bottom and center cup when they are placed mouth down, and put the three large balls or potatoes in the right coat pocket. You will also need something for a wand. This can be a piece of dowel rod about one half inch in diameter and a foot long painted to look like your idea of a wand. Place the remaining three small balls in your servante, which should be located so you can secure the balls in the act of picking up the wand from the table.

Show your hands empty, pick up the cups and do the galloping post move several times. Place the cups on the table in a row, leaving a ball under the center cup, unknown to the audience. Pick up the wand, securing at the same time one of the small balls, which you hold concealed in the hand that holds the wand. Tap the center cup with the wand, lift it with the left hand, revealing one ball. Put down the wand, near the servante, transfer the cup in the left hand to the right hand and pick up the visible ball with the left hand. Replace the cup in position, secretly dropping the ball palmed in the right hand under it.

Place the ball in the left hand on top of the center cup. Raise the right hand cup with the right hand and put this cup on top of the center one, over the ball on top of the cup.

Lift the two cups, showing that the ball has penetrated the cup. Then put the top cup down in the right hand position, in a manner similar to the galloping post move, thereby placing a concealed ball under the right-hand cup. This leaves you with one cup in the left hand. Pick up the left-hand cup with the right hand and perform the penetration of one cup by the other.

Then put the cup in the right hand on the visible ball. Pick up the wand, securing another ball from the servante. Tap the right-hand cup with the wand and tip it over with the wand. Lay down the wand, near the servante, and transfer the cup in the left hand to the right hand, tipping it forward when it is held in the right hand and inserting the ball in the right hand secretly into the cup. Put this cup down in the left-hand position while tipping the center cup, with the left hand revealing another ball. Pick up the wand with the right hand, securing another ball. Tap the left-hand cup with the wand, lay down the wand and pick up the left-hand cup with the right hand, revealing another ball.

Put the cup in the right hand back on top of this ball, dropping the concealed ball in this cup to join the visible one that is being covered. Pick up the ball in front of the center cup and apparently place it under the cup while righting the cup, actually retaining the ball in the hand. Pick up the last visible ball and place it under the right-hand cup together with the palmed ball as the cup is righted. Pick up the wand and tap the center cup, asking which one of the end cups the spectator would prefer. Tap the one he selects with the wand and tip it over. Then tip the center cup over with the wand. The ball in the center has apparently traveled to the end cup. Lay down the wand, pick up the two visible balls and apparently place them under the end cup previously overturned, actually palming one of them and placing the other under the cup.

Right the center cup with the left hand, pick up the wand in the right, and tap the other end cup to show that the ball could have equally well been conjured into it. Tip the cup and show that there are two balls under it. Tip the end cup selected originally by the spectator and show that it now contains but one ball. Lay down wand, raise center cup with right hand to show it empty, in replacing drop concealed ball under. Pick up one of the three visible balls, the ones which were under the end cups, and place it on top of the center cup. Stack one of the other two cups on the center one and lift the two to show that the ball on top has apparently penetrated the center cup. By placing the upper cup over the ball that just penetrated in the swinging motion of the galloping post move, the concealed ball is added to the visible one and another ball is placed on top of the cup. Again a cup is stacked on the cup just placed down and another ball is seen to have penetrated. Repeat this move with the last visible ball.

You now have two cups with a ball between and three balls showing. Put the three visible balls in a row and put one cup over each, catching the ball between the two cups in the finger palm position in the right hand when separating the two cups to set them down. Raise the right hand cup with the right hand and pick up the ball with the left hand. Replace the cup, dropping the palmed ball under it. Transfer the ball in the left hand to the right and put the right hand in the right coat pocket, palming the ball while lifting the center cup with the left hand. Transfer the cup to the right hand and pick up the ball with the left. Place the cup down, dropping the palmed ball under it. Transfer the ball in the left hand to the right which again goes to the pocket, palming the ball while the left hand raises another cup to disclose a ball. This may be repeated as long as desired to show a multiplication of balls, since each time one is picked up the previous one is being replaced under the cup just raised.

Continue the process as long as your sense of timing tells you is desirable and then each time the hand goes into the pocket, drop one of the small balls and pick up a large one, until all three large ones have been transferred to the cups. Finish by turning over the three cups to reveal the three large balls.

Bibliography

History—Background

Autobiographies of Conjurers:
Bertram, Charles. *Isn't It Wonderful?* London, Swan Sonnenschein & Co., 1899.
———. *A Magician in Many Lands.* London, George Routledge & Sons, 1911.
Blitz, Signor. *The Life and Adventures of Signor Blitz.* Hartford, 1872.
Devant, David. *Woes of a Wizard.* London, S. H. Bousfield & Co., 1903.
Hertz, Carl. *A Modern Mystery Merchant.* London, Hutchinson & Co., 1924.
Maskelyne, Jasper. *White Magic.* London, Stanley Paul & Co., 1936.
Robert-Houdin. *King of the Conjurers.* New York, Dover Publications, 1964.
Scarne, John. *The Odds Against Me.* New York, Simon & Schuster, 1966.
Thurston, Howard. *My Life of Magic.* Philadelphia, Dorrance & Co., 1929.

Gambling Exposés by Magicians:
Erdnase, S. W. *The Expert at the Card Table.* Chicago, Frederick J. Drake & Co., 1934.
MacDougall, Michael. *Gamblers Don't Gamble.* New York, The Greystone Press, 1939.

211

Maskelyne, John Nevil. *Sharps and Flats*. London, Longmans, Green, & Co., 1894.

Robert-Houdin, J. E. *Card Sharpers*. London, Spencer Blackett, 1891.

Scarne, John. *Scarne on Cards*. New York, Crown Publishers, 1965.

————. *Scarne on Dice*. Harrisburg, Pa., The Military Service Publishing Co., 1945.

History:

Boston, George L. *Inside Magic*. New York, The Beechhurst Press.

Brewster, Sir David. *Letters on Natural Magic*. London, John Murray and Thomas Tegg, 1838.

Burlingame, H. J. *Herrmann the Great*. Chicago, Albert Whitman & Co., 1897.

Chapuis, Alfred and Edmond Droz. *Automata*. New York, Central Book Company, Editions du Griffon, 1958.

Christopher, Milbourne. *Panorama of Magic*. New York, Dover Publications, 1962.

Dexter, Will. *The Riddle of Chung Ling Soo*. London, Arco Publishers, 1955.

Dexter, Will. *This is Magic*. London, Arco Publications Ltd., 1958.

Evans, Henry Ridgely. *History of Conjuring and Magic*. Kenton, Ohio, International Brotherhood of Magicians, 1928.

————. *The Old and the New Magic*. Chicago, The Open Court Publishing Co., 1909.

Frost, Thomas. *Lives of the Conjurers*. London, Chatto & Windus, 1881.

Gibson, Walter. *The Master Magicians*. New York, Doubleday & Co., 1966.

Goldston, Will. *Sensational Tales of Mystery Men*. London, Will Goldston Ltd., 1929.

Gresham, William Lindsay. *Houdini—The Man Who Walked Through Walls*. New York, Chicago, San Francisco, Holt, Rinehart & Winston, 1959.

Hocus Pocus Junior (Reprint of 1675 edition). New York, John McArdle, 1950.

Hopkins, Albert A. *Magic, Stage Illusions, & Scientific Diversions*. New York, Munn & Co., 1901.

Houdini, Harry. *The Unmasking of Robert-Houdin.* New York, The Publishers Printing Co., 1908.

Ireland, Frances. *You Don't Have to be Crazy.* Chicago, Ireland Magic Co., 1946.

Kellock, Harold. *Houdini.* New York, Harcourt, Brace & Co., 1928.

Mulholland, John. *Quicker Than the Eye.* Indianapolis, Bobbs-Merrill Co., 1932.

Salverte, Eusebe. *The Philosophy of Magic,* Vol. 1 & Vol. 2. New York, Harper & Brothers, 1855.

Sardina, Maurice. *Where Houdini Was Wrong.* London, George Armstrong, 1950.

Severn, Bill. *Magic and Magicians.* New York, David McKay Company, 1958.

Zolotow, Maurice. *It Takes All Kinds.* New York, Random House, 1952.

Psychology of Conjuring:

Fitzkee, Dariel. *Showmanship for Magicians.* San Rafael, California, Saint Raphael House, 1945.

――――. *Magic by Misdirection.* San Rafael, California, Saint Raphael House, 1945.

――――. *The Trick Brain.* San Rafael, California, Saint Rafael House, 1944.

Gregory, R. L. *Eye and Brain, The Psychology of Seeing.* New York, Toronto, McGraw-Hill Book Co., 1966.

Maskelyne, N. and D. Devant. *Our Magic.* Berkeley Heights, New Jersey, Fleming Book Co., 1946.

Sharpe, S. H. *Neo Magic.* London, George Johnson, 1946.

――――. *Good Conjuring.* London, George Johnson, 1936.

――――. *Conjured Up.* London, George Johnson, 1935.

Triplett, Norman. *The Psychology of Conjuring Deceptions.* The American Journal of Psychology, Vol. IX, No. 4, July, 1900.

Spirit Exposés by Magicians:

Abbott, David P. *Behind the Scenes with the Medium.* Chicago, The Open Court Publishing Co., 1926.

Chislett. *Spirits in the House.* Birmingham, England, Goodliffe, 1949.

Dunninger, Joseph. *How to Make a Ghost Walk.* New York, David Kemp & Co., 1936.

Dunninger, Joseph. *Inside the Medium's Cabinet.* New York, David Kemp & Co., 1935.

Mulholland, John. *Beware Familiar Spirits.* New York, Charles Scribner's Sons, 1938.

MAGIC TRICKS

A = Beginner
B = Intermediate
C = Expert

Card Fanning:

Love, Edward G. *Card Fan-Tasies.* London, 1964. B

Dodson, Goodlette. *Exhibition Card Fans.* Atlanta, Georgia, Atlanta Magic Co., 1935. B

Cups and Balls:

Farelli, Victor. *John Ramsay's Routine with Cups and Balls.* London, George Armstrong, 1948. B-C

Ganson, Lewis. *The Dai Vernon Cups and Balls.* B

Ireland, Laurie. *Ireland's Original Cup and Ball Routines.* Chicago, Ireland Magic Co., 1961. A-B

Joseph, Eddie. *The Last Word on Cups and Balls.* Colon, Michigan, Abbott's Magic Novelty Co., 1942. B

————. *The Hindu Cups.* London, Max Andrews Ltd. B

Osborne, Tom. *Cups and Balls Magic.* Philadelphia, Kanter's Magic Shop, 1937. A-B

General Magic:

Bamberg, Theodore. *Okito on Magic.* Chicago, Edward O. Drane & Co., 1952. B-C

Curry, Paul. *Magician's Magic.* New York, Franklin Watts, Inc., 1965. A

Devant, David. *Secrets of My Magic.* London, Hutchinson & Co., 1936. B-C

Downs, T. Nelson. *The Art of Magic.* Chicago, Arthur P. Felsman, 1921. B-C

Fischer, Ottokar. *Illustrated Magic.* New York, The Macmillan Co., 1936. A

Hilliard, John Northern. *Greater Magic.* Minneapolis, Carl Waring Jones, 1938. A-B-C

Hoffmann, Professor. *Modern Magic*. London & Manchester, George Routledge and Sons, 1878. A-B

——. *More Magic*. London, Glasgow and Manchester, George Routledge and Sons, 1889. A-B

——. *Later Magic*. New York, E. P. Dutton & Co., 1935. A-B

Mulholland, John. *Magic of the World*. New York, Charles Scribner's Sons, 1965. A

Neil, C. Lang. *The Modern Conjurer*. New York, David Kemp & Co., 1937. B

Rice, Harold R. *Encyclopedia of Silk Magic*, Vols. 1 to 3. Wynnewood, Pennsylvania, Silk King Studios, 1948-1962. B-C

Robert-Houdin, J. E. *The Secrets of Conjuring and Magic*. London, George Routledge and Sons, 1877.

Sharpe, S. H. *Ponsin on Conjuring*. London, George Johnson, 1937. C

Tarbell, Harlan. *Tarbell Course in Magic*, Vols. 1 to 6. New York, Louis Tannen, 1941-1954. A-B-C

Self Working Tricks:

Blackstone, Harry. *Modern Card Tricks and Secrets of Magic*. New York, Garden City Publishing Co., 1941. A

Clive, Paul. *Card Tricks Without Skill*. London, Faber and Faber, 1959. A-B

Elliott, Bruce. *Magic as a Hobby*. New York, Harper & Brothers, 1948. B

Gardner, Martin. *Mathematics, Magic and Mystery*. New York, Dover Publications, 1956. A-B

Hugard, Jean. *Encyclopedia of Card Tricks*. New York, Max Holden, 1937. A-B

Scarne, John. *Scarne on Card Tricks*. New York, Crown Publishers, 1950. A-B

Thurston, Howard. *200 Tricks You Can Do*. New York, George Sully & Co., 1926. A

Sleight of Hand:

Bobo, J. B. *Modern Coin Magic*. Minneapolis, Carl W. Jones, 1952. A-B-C

Buckley, Arthur. *Card Control*. Springfield, Illinois, Arthur H. Buckley, 1946. B-C

Chanin, Jack. *Grand Finale*. Philadelphia, Jack Chanin, 1952. B

Downs, T. Nelson. *Tricks with Coins*. New York, Wehman Bros., 1905. B-C

Farelli, Victor. *Convincing Coin Magic*. London, George Armstrong, 1946. A-B

Gaultier, Camille. *Magic Without Apparatus*. Berkeley Heights, New Jersey, 1945. A-B-C

Ganson, Lewis. *The Dai Vernon Book of Magic*. London, Harry Stanley. B-C

————. *The Magic of Slydini*. London, Harry Stanley. B-C

————. *Routined Manipulation Finale*. London, Harry Stanley. B-C

Hugard, Jean. *Card Manipulations*, Vols. 1 to 5. New York, Max Holden. B-C

————. *More Card Manipulations*, Vols. 1 to 4. New York, Max Holden. B-C

————. *Expert Card Technique*. Minneapolis, Carl Waring Jones, 1940. C

Hull, Burling. *Expert Billiard Ball Manipulation*, Vol. 1 and Vol. 2. New York, Stage Magic Co., 1928. C

James, Stewart. *Abbott's Encyclopedia of Rope Tricks*. Colon, Michigan, Percy Abbott, 1945. A-B-C

Lorayne, Harry. *Close-Up Card Magic*. New York, Louis Tannen, 1962. B-C

Ortmann, Otto. *The Physiological Mechanics of Piano Technique*. New York, E. P. Dutton & Co., 1962.

Sachs, Edwin T. *Sleight of Hand*. Berkeley Heights, New Jersey, Fleming Book Co., 1946. A-B

Starke, George (ed.). *Stars of Magic*. New York, Stars of Magic, Inc., 1947-1952. B-C

Thurston, Howard. *50 New Card Tricks*. New York, Wehman Brothers, 1905. B

Vernon, Dai. *Malini and His Magic*. London, Harry Stanley. B-C

Victor, Edward. *The Magic of the Hands*. England, Waddilove & Co. Ltd. B-C